AMAROMA EDICIONES

HOUSES BY THE SEA

And these places are just waiting for us to take a look...

RAÚL ACEVES

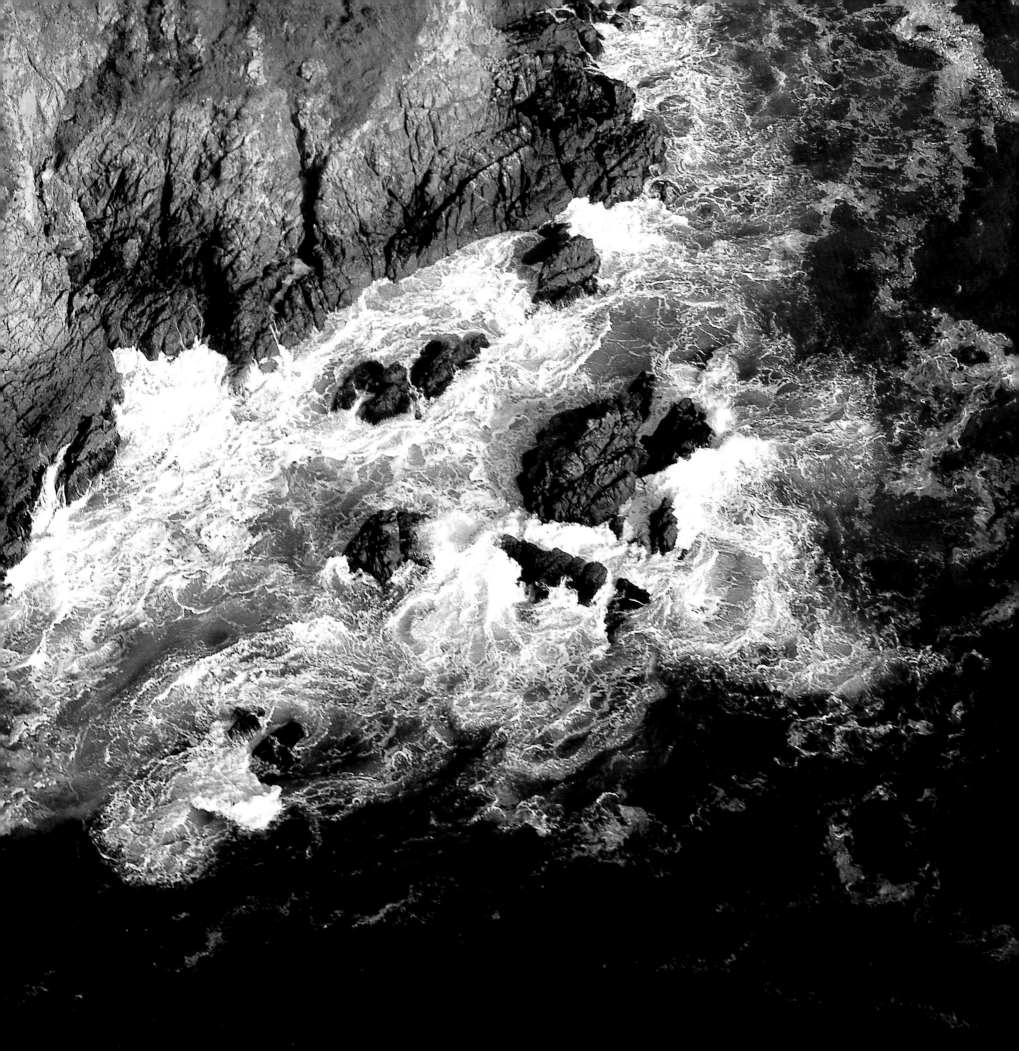

AMAROMA EDICIONES

HOUSES BY THE SEA

PUBLISHING PROJECT DIRECTOR MAURICIO MARTÍNEZ   PHOTOGRAPHY RIGOBERTO MORENO   TEXTS ALICIA ALDRETE

A t the edge of the sea, upon barren rock, among vegetation that seems to wrap it in a wall of green, under a sky that opens to let mighty clouds pass at will, rises the house.

A house constructed meticulously, piece by piece at the hands of masters, it is a dream materialized thanks to the judicious exercise of choice and patience. More than that, it is a dream in which one can live. Its spaces have been designed for human delight. What better rationale could there be for tangible reverie?

Placed on a lovingly-selected site facing the vast ocean, it quietly sounds the first line of a dialogue with the landscape. Open, it is a refuge which grants entrance to the best of the day's sun and wind. There are birds that descend to drink bits of sky from the pools. Closed and nocturnal, it is an observatory for watching the rotation of the stars. Still, the sea arranges things so that it can slip into bedrooms like a dark and mysterious rumor.

Sometimes, sheltered by the mountain, the house is transformed: it is a mirror for the sounds of the jungle. A light flowery notation is lavished upon the eyes, and the air on the terraces fills with the plain racket of insects and birds. Other times, the house seems to have sprung like an apparition from amidst round and jagged rocks. The desert surrounds it with the deceptive calm of a sleeping animal: a truce must then be negotiated with the expanse of golden sands.

Isolated, enclosed or open, along a coast that might think itself unconquerable, each house unfolds its structure, like a rare variety of earthly flower turning toward the majestic power of the sea.

Jorge Esquinca

HOUSES BY THE SEA

Published by: AMAROMA EDICIONES,
Av. Vallarta 1835-2, Col. Americana,
44140 Guadalajara, Jalisco, México
Tel. (33) 36 16 53 43 Fax (33) 36 16 53 46
E-MAIL: amaroma@vinet.com.mx
amaroma@prodigy.net.mx

Hardcover Spanish Edition: ISBN 970-92410-6-0
Hardcover English Edition: ISBN 970-92410-7-9
Printed in Hong Kong by *Global Interprint, Inc.*

DESIGN
Mauricio Martínez Rosas
Rocío Guillén Solís

EXECUTIVE PRODUCTION
Amaroma Ediciones

SUPERVISED EDITORS
Augusta Cobar
Rocío Guillén Solís

TEXTUAL CONSULTANT
Michael Hogan

TRANSLATION
Lucinda Mayo

PRE-PRESS
Groppe

H abitat and architecture seem to be questions of universal interest. Each of us either dreams about, imagines or actually owns a house upon which we project our way of life and our feelings. It is our home, the place that contains and preserves the most highly-regarded values, as well as the main elements of culture.

Just as universally, the sea holds a constant attraction for us. Whether stretching alongside sunstruck deserts or exuberant tropics, the sea always represents a mythical destination towards which our steps are drawn, a place where the horizon is blue and infinite. In those who encounter it, it provokes a wave of archaic sensations, perhaps derived from our first memories. Maybe this is why a house by the sea has long been seen by many as an ideal place to live, or to at least spend a long sojourn. Examples of this ideal exist all along the length of Mexico's Pacific coast.

In an architecture borne of multiple influences and inexhaustible vitality, in the most impressive settings this geography affords, a dialogue takes place – between the forces of nature and constructed areas. Houses by the Sea narrates some of the stories that arise from that exchange.

Traditional materials and processes are used concurrently with the highest and most sophisticated contemporary technology, making these houses pieces of an intricate cultural mosaic, bringing together exotic and sensual treasures. The pages of this book recount the manner in which we build, and show the great capacity, quality and skill that characterize the most renowned Mexican workmanship.

Combining Rigoberto Moreno's excellent images with Alicia Aldrete's eloquent words, Houses by the Sea endeavors to convey an overview of these dreams...come true.

MAURICIO MARTÍNEZ ROSAS

CASA *Chololo*

EDWARD Y FRANCIS BAROW
OWNERS

ARCHITECT RUBÉN ÁLVAREZ IBARRA
ARCHITECT ENRIQUE GARCÍA ÁLVAREZ
PROJECT

On thirty-two acres there rise two small structures, on two levels. The owners asked the architects if they could use this pair of rooms as a temporary home while the estate was being constructed, and later turn them into guest bungalows. And as the client is always right, the answer was affirmative. Thus began the story of Casa Chololo: with the humble task of relocating the bats who inhabited the gables of the two buildings.

The goals of Edward, the owner, were very clear. Not to have neighbors nearby, and to absolutely respect the natural world. Not terribly difficult to accomplish, because the estate is «big enough» – to put it mildly – and because the trees of the region come in wonderful shapes and sizes.

He tells us that with an estate like Chololo, there is the risk of designing a magnificent showplace which makes the residents feel they are always on stage. However, Álvarez and García (AG Arquitectos) work «by basic instinct» to construct a real world in which human beings are comfortable.

Facing the sea

«By respecting the two rooms that were already here, and given the height of the jungle clearing where they stood, the living room could have could have had an unimpeded view of the sea. But no: we turned it, breaking up the vista. Why? A quick look provides the answer: focussing on just one-third of the panorama offers the house not only ocean and beach outlooks, but a part of the scenery from the tree-covered hills. «You don't get too far from the earth: you stay in touch with the land, and it gives you a feeling of sanctuary.» This decision confers a special personality on the house, not in an obvious way, but in a subtle

This is the result of a plan that has hurled itself into space, showing how dazzling ideas can be when they take on physical reality.

and ethereal one. We don't need to know why; the mood is just different. Watching the sunset from the terrace of Chololo House is like late-afternoon in any other magnificent place by the sea, but here there is inexplicably more: having a ribbon of mountain and lush foliage enter our field of vision is a rich counterpoint to the impression of waves eternally splashing on the shore.

When all is said and done

Helplessly drawn to the entrance patio by its carefully-focussed view, we climb the wide steps to stand before a set of double doors. They seem heavy with age; but the two panels can be dramatically flung open to the world, or a smaller visual vignette may be created by leaving one panel shut.

Nature's wall, nature's roof

The potential for interlopers from the wild is hardly a minor concern, but their presence provides no threat: nature is invited to become part of the household. In this area, the tones of the hemp ropes that fasten palapas, the shades of the *guayabillo* tree-trunks used in the construction, the colors of palm leaves; all are captured and reproduced. Down below, the harmonious hues of a coastal sunset are brought into play.

At Chololo everything is real, there are no artificial versions of nature, and nothing that tries to improve upon its perfection. Everything we see has a function, a reason and purpose. Also, reality is adjustable: the winds, the sun, the view, can all be varied to fit personal desires, according to the time of day. This is one of the fundamental rules of the game these architects played, but they were not alone. «Edward Barow was instrumental in the project's success: sensitive, respectful, creative and open to suggestions,» Enrique emphatically assures us.

Like a hermit crab

Inside we find a short, but very tall, palapa-topped hallway: to the left turning into a bridge, and to the right a staircase - which spirals along the wall until it reaches the lower level. To describe it all requires a bit of eloquence: the conical palm roof, supported by a circular concrete structure, rises almost fify feet above the ground; the very apogee of the vestibule. A *chololo* or hermit crab living in a snail shell – one of many who reside in the region – graces the floor, enclosed in circular stone borders. A huge potted palm completes the spectacular scene.

The sea, the mountain and the sky
stand by, permanent companions
for the «hermit crab» in its new locale.

«In spite of its dimensions, the space does not seem out of proportion, because it encompasses two levels.» And it follows the architects' initial premise: to cherish the sensation of well-being and refuge for the human residents, without sacrificing an almost complete communion with the natural world outside.

The bridge leads to a bedroom – one of the original ones, which forgets its rustic past and takes on a new character, facing both landscapes and seascapes. This is considered the master bedroom: at the same level as the entrance, it is also «the highest on the property, its ceiling rising over all the others.» Its earlier twin, while on a lower plane, is «right up there» in terms of comfort, luxury, design, and view: both have outdoor bathrooms – of granite which recaptures its natural stone identity –, impertinent as they bare themselves to the world. Sinks, showers and jacuzzis are unabashed; only the WC is enclosed. A daring proposition which doesn't view privacy in the most conventional sense, but nevertheless safeguards a sense of intimacy.

Standing behind the house, the hill is a backdrop full of earth-tones, and lush with vegetation. The plant-life, much of it spilling forth in a riot of green, is native to the property: only here it lives better, with more care and more frequent watering.

Taking turns

From the vestibule the dining room opens up, and in this house the verb-phrase «open up» leaves no room for confusion. Here there is a certain Thai feeling to the triangle of palapa that ends in a peaked roof. Living room, terrace, and a swimming pool which came to life as a rediscovery of curvilinear forms.

To one side, a staircase – which recalls the circular forms of the entranceway – curls down into the «The Pasha's Bedroom», as Francis Barow calls it. This area was not originally part of the plan, but occurred through a kind of on-site «fieldwork» that paid attention to the actual demands of the terrain and the existing surroundings.

Now it is a bedroom that distances itself from the everyday world and merges with the view. The energy of wild vegetation, the power of the ocean tides, are concentrated here in an elegant hideaway.

We could say that the terrace is a gift from the swimming pool, the roof from the living room, and the jacuzzi from a play of watery depths that mirror the ocean it views from a high, narrow window. And the *chololo* never left, it's all dressed up in its best attire, and stays just where it belongs.

With perfect ratio of humility and pride,
the house makes itself at home in the landscape.

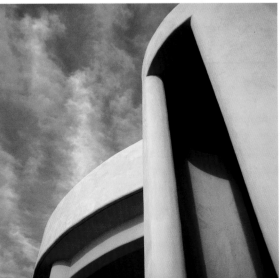

Las Gaviotas

Casa Las Gaviotas:
Audacity that makes sense of space

Don and Alice Willfong
OWNERS

Architect Juan Manuel Munguía
PROJECT

Juan Pablo Stone
CONSTRUCTION

Jean Philippe Armenta
LANDSCAPE

Architecture is an adventure shared by client and architect, in equal measure. «For the adventure to become a work of art, mutual understanding must develop on many levels: intellectual, aesthetic, emotional and cultural. When that is achieved, the result is a very pleasing one,» Juan Manuel Munguía assures us, and Las Gaviotas, the house named for the soaring flight of seagulls, attests to the fact that his statement is not merely words.

And if that relationship doesn't grow, he adds, the stronger elements win; either the financial power and cultural obstinacy of the owner, or the craft – and craftiness – of the architect.

This house is completely candid about the way in which owners' and architect's interests came together, and about the geometry that was their focus. Instead of hiding these, it accentuates them: there is no trepidation about straight lines, circular forms nor expansive surfaces; neither is there any shyness about honoring whoever came up with a particular plan. There is a sense of composition, of space and form and freedom, without blushing at the idea of emulating, interpreting, or evoking. The shared adventure has been a success. «I believe in the forces of geometry, and in the forces of light.»

Juan Manuel says that in addition to the participation of the client and the architect, there is another determining factor for success: the land. «Las Gaviotas is placed on the brink of a cliff almost seventy feet high – a nearly vertical rock face – with a natural presence so strong that it might make anyone nervous

Not a patio that looks out to sea, but which has the indulgence and effrontery to be a completely private space - lulled by the waves' measured rhythm from afar.

about playing with it, trying to imitate it.» The site itself dictates, and depends upon the sensitivity of the people involved to listen to its dictates, not to turn a deaf ear.

Angular stone

The jumping-off point for the project was a dream Don had, in which he imagined the remains of an old hacienda, lost and rediscoved on the site where Las Gaviotas now stands. «The challenge was to construct this image using contemporary forms and systems, without losing its essence.» With this in mind, the central patio, «while not confined within elements of symmetry, achieves balance through a series of architectural traditions,» in a free, assymetrical composition that is completed by the garden. «The landscaping has a very strong formal *raison d'être*, which was foreseen from the project's beginning.»

The house extends a bold welcome, which engages the spirit of anyone who crosses its threshold: here there is an intimate patio, with a very long swimming pool – so isolated from the ocean that one simply intuits its presence by listening to the sounds of the surf. «This is not the first time that I have kept the the ocean from taking center-stage; I consider curiosity and mystery to be necessary ingredients in this life. And the coastal landscape is so generous, so wide, that if we did not enclose it in a kind of shadow box, a frame of reference, it would vanish, escape, get lost. Or it might become overwhelming: controlling it is our arquitectural task.»

At the end of the patio rises a rectangular mass of stone, reaching towards the sky. Everything about it speaks of gracefulness, and everything around it: the doorway, the palm trees on both sides, the metal lanterns.

Its presence alone is imposing, its power displayed when the two heavy wooden doors are opened and the ocean appears within their sturdy frame. There at the end of the property, before it reaches the water, is a triangular swimming pool – shaped like the prow of a ship – that seems about to launch itself in the bay.

This is the central motif of the structure; recalling the old hacienda from Don's dream, but speaking in its own language. The owners are sensitive enough to find a spiritual voyage within this economy of forms.

Along the interior patio, with its extended swimming pool, the library rises unhesitatingly, in the shape of a cross: with two entrances to the garden, two windows, and a central area topped

With neither a competitive spirit
nor an imitation of nature's riches, this house
is simply energized by its surroundings.

by a pyramid. The hallway is an open palapa, its wicker window treatments tied with rawhide. A cleanly-designed staircase leads to the second floor bedroom. It is evident that the owners know and collect art, and such details are simply more clues to their character.

Healthy tension

Within the main room, volume is accompanied by simplicity. This area has two moods, one introverted and the other directed outdoors. «It had to convey an important sense of undivided space, but on the other hand, the demands of life in this climate required that it be partly covered, and partly exposed.»

They chose an invisible material, the airiest possible. «The glass works well, but it had to be structured in a special way.» They opted for a web of stainless steel and tension cables to hold the twenty-four pieces in place, «always with the goal of its being barely visible, but also having the responsibility of supporting this transparent membrane.»

The ceiling is profusely decorated with uninterrupted geometric design, «the glass appearing as if by accident, with its shapes and tones lending a sense of playfulness.» The stone staircase – together with the doorway, palm trees and lanterns – is a tribute to verticality, an invitation to gaze upward and allow one's spirit to be enraptured by color.

Decoration

«Architecture consists in spaces, and decorating them is what aligns them with man; it makes aesthetic enjoyment possible.» Thus the architect felt it necessary to participate in the design of the furnishings, and the forms he developed were also geometric: pure, proportioned, vintage. He had them made in mezquite, and they pay homage to the wood itself; conceptual inertia which transcends the inner environment and restrains decorative objects.

«Man is the great protagonist, and this is how we ought to view architecture; to such a degree that the décor must speak of meeting the residents' every need.» This house has no empty spots whatsoever, and lacks nothing.

«Quality of life does need to be accompanied by many things; we each carry an experience of vitality within us, in our spirit and intellect.» As Juan Manuel understands architecture, «The fewer the distractions, the greater possibility there is of experiencing that life force.»

The language of the home's interior
is simple and discriminating,
and serves a particular function – nothing more.

VILLA *Vista Mágica*

With its circular plan, the house is an ever-changing excursion. A collection of uncommon elements, spaces emerging whimsically, circumferences framed to wrap the view and appropriate the ocean all for themselves. The goodness of a place that desires nothing but to accommodate John Hardesty's ideas, to see them brought to life upon its soil. A permanent rehearsal space, with independence and confidence to do whatever comes to mind on this land, in this doting weather and with this privileged perspective.

Hardesty is a businessman with a natural vocation for creativity. Having had his own precise concept for a house on the beach in Mexico, what he needed was someone to put his yearnings on paper, and then to transform them into walls, ceilings and floors.

Tatiana Borioli became the lucky translator of those dreams, in charge of placing them on this actual property. The result is a mix of magic that speaks different languages, fed by the cultures of Mexico's diverse regions.

Villa Vista Mágica (Magical View) has permission to take colors and shapes from wherever it likes, and it likes to refer to folk tradition,

archaeology, indigenous textiles. It is an homage to what is Mexican, and takes a respectful but festive approach, with a sense of always searching, emulating, and drawing upon inspiration.

Thatched palapas and circular forms are the constants here, with all the different versions of these that the imagination can devise. In its generosity, the estate allows a thousand facades without their colliding, or contradicting one another: massive walls in bougainvillea colors facing narrow wooden fencing; squat leather furniture under an incredibly tall palapa; murals in some areas, blank walls in others; a lonely bench on an overlook versus profusely furnished rooms; railings of cane tied with hemp, on balconies with curving metal frames and shining glass windowpanes.

The only things that Vista Mágica has no room for are bashfulness, subjection to conventional schemes, or blocks to creativity – whether they have to do with emotions, structural constraints, or color theory.

The map

Tatiana says that the term «magic» in the house's name was taken almost directly from the cosmic vision of Mexico's ethnic groups. She divided the country into regions and borrowed from five indigenous groups: in the states of Puebla, Oaxaca, Michoacán and Guanajuato, and from her main inspiration, strongly reminiscent of the Huichol people who live in a mountainous corner that crosses several state borders in western Mexico.

She adds that the principle uniting the project is the circle, the sun, and that all is embraced by this form. It is present in the

In such a magical view there is no room
for limitations on form; imagination,
fantasy and contrast are the currency of the realm.

footpaths, the baths and bedrooms, in all the décor. The pool is graced by a circle in lively colors, which the Jacuzzi repeats in the brash reds of a full sunset.

Each of the suites is rounded, with thatch ceilings and curving windows. John proudly demonstrates a window and takes full credit for its success. «They told me it wasn't possible, and they were so sure of it,» but there are his windows, they open and close easily, and can be hidden so that the structure may return to its more primitive state.

Every bathroom is a proposal in graphic design and engineering: the tiles and sinks are designed to order, there are eight showers so as not to chance anyone being unable to get wet when they'd like – and this along with the infrastructure that is required for all eight to provide good water pressure.

Tatiana remembers the experience of traveling from one town to another in search of the best artisans to create the motifs that would grace the ceramics. These would later be reproduced in the cabinetry, which would take on the same colors and forms. She also recalls that a drafting table was brought out to the building site so that modifications could be made to the plans while the work was in progress: to open a window wider, to frame the view more effectively, to close a niche or raise a ceiling.

Nothing in Vista Mágica gets far from the principle of playfulness imprinted upon the house by John, who proudly walks through his home and pauses, as if for the first time, to notice the details with which it is filled, and which give him such satisfaction.

Architecturally as well as decoratively,
the project enjoys total freedom,
obeys only its master's voice, and adapts itself
to his commands. The results are self-evident.

Tasting and Testing

The plot of land, located on a rocky cliff between two gorgeous beaches, is enormous. There had already been a building here, with right angles and views interrupted by thick pillars: now nothing remains of those past features. In their place are open spaces, and lighthearted – but huge – palapas. The communal palapa has a bar, two dining areas, and who knows how many other seating arrangements. The kitchen is hidden away on the floor below, along with ample pantries and storerooms.

John and Clara's suite is grand and spacious as well, but the lines of its walls are also completely clean and unfussy. It has no curved windows, but pieces of glass held by narrow pillars and wooden columns – the same as in the palm-leaf structure. It contains a living room, dining room, kitchen and study. The bath is an extension of the bedroom, as is the terrace. The furniture here also declares its freedom, and everything including the air conditioning equipment is tinted with color.

The Guanajuato villa is decorated with talavera ceramics. The one dedicated to Michoacán is full of fish and butterflies: not just in brush-strokes or flashes of color, but with the full intent of chasing away worries and creating a mini-cosmos that is at once determined and playful. Clara interjects to tell us that the surface of the principal driveway gave them some difficulty, because there was a risk of cars slipping on it during the rainy season, and how it occurred to John to simply reverse the way the paving was set, and thus solve the problem.

History

John wanders through his property back to the time in his memory when the work was still under way. He's glad to see a high wall that has two painted fish as its principal decoration, and another depicting the Aztec calendar, polished cement with sparkling colors that were added by a group of friends during a party. He enters the baths and is pleased by their combinations of tones, and the placement of their fixtures. His frank laughter is heard as he shows a mirror – framed by a stained glass window – over one of the beds. And the owner's delight can be simply explained: customized design encompasses everything, from closet doors to dinnerware and cupboards. And he is the author of all that he sees.

The site could not be better:
a rise between two expanses of lovely beachfront.
View is everything. Greenery is abundant. Luxury?
Only that which is deemed necessary.

CASA LA ESCONDIDA:
IT APPEARS WITHOUT WARNING,
AND CREATES SURPRISE
AS A MATTER OF COURSE

ARCHITECT PRÓSPERO TAPIA
PROJECT

PROTIP
CONSTRUCTION

Viewed from its entrance it manages to be subtle, but not entirely unobtrusive. The first detail we see is the gate embellished with bits of blue glass, which will take on more meaning later, when we visit the interior of the house.

And it might also seem a tranquil edifice, when we are looking at it from the carport area. «It stands here, proper and unpretentious.» The most interesting things happen on the lower level, where La Escondida, the «Hidden House», is actually located.

Pure magic
In making their descent, the stairs are escorted by rolling gardens. A kind of cylindrical millstone then appears: not announcing itself, it demands that the visitor really look for it; but then it becomes a strong and slightly «in your face» presence.

«What it is, is a kind of palm tree that has turned to a pillar of stone, taking the design of what it finds beside it and duplicating that on a grand scale: an organic tower that has stolen the texture of the tree trunk,» is how Próspero Tapia begins to describe the forms of La Escondida's entranceway.

«With its deep frame and tall narrow doorway, the foyer is reminiscent of medieval style, adapted to Mexican Modern.» The interior is finished with a vaulted ceiling, and its floor is adorned with a «rug» of inlaid stone.

Prospero Tapia likes to use several elements as constants throughout his construction process, which lends continuity, and «grounds» the design. In this home he used rounded stones in an unsuspected place: as a kind of picture rail just below the ceiling. «This high dado provides design integrity, with energy running through it from one space to another.»

The building is hidden away, so as not to challenge the setting with its forms, nor to scandalize any visual conventions. It succeeds in this, of course, but only to a degree.

Ceilings and subtleties

«Spatial fantasy,» is what Tapia considers his calling, and the house abounds with its manifestations. «The environment sets the mood, and from there the house's character is born: formality when required, spaciousness when necessary.»

From a narrow hallway we come upon an generous and ample living room. Here Tapia's ceilings provide the residents with visual clues. The one in the dining room is made of wooden staves in a squared-off design, placed exactly over the round table; the library's has its own neighboring version; the terrace – which appears to be part of the interior, but is not – has another texture, another design, even another color, and it seems to float, not to enclose but nevertheless to shelter. The television room has a high ceiling, and there we see the blue glass panes again, in a large stained-glass window that not only encompasses two storeys but incorporates the living room's upper floor. This impressive window is treated almost like an icon, and it shares materials with the entrance hall's doorframe as a means of interrelating the two spaces.

«I always look for a continuity between areas, defined by the ceilings: proportion, functionality, aesthetics, views. Often it is a pretext for creating a framework, at other times it becomes a strong defining element which offers a feeling of security and ensures that no one spends too much time in any one place, but pushes them to explore other areas.

As simple as can be

«New spaces have been created so that one discovers various kinds of ambience when one enters the house. When you leave the pool, tired of the sun, you have the pleasant surprise of being able to sit down in front of the TV, or to relax in the most sociable part of the kitchen.»

The terrace, for example, resolves the exterior-interior conundrum by taking the strong winds into account, then molding and tempering them into a setting for ease and well-being. Across the way it has sliding doors outfitted with mosquito netting. Where it adjoins the dining room, panels of wood with inset windows offer rooms the opportunity to provide one another with natural air conditioning. On one of its walls, there are two images that are the very opposite of «still lifes» – foliage seen through each of the windows flanking the barbecue, masterpieces of balance and coloration.

The central space flows without apparent restraints, free all along its length and width. But it is indefinite enough to include all the elements necessary for dividing and devising itself so that every area benefits from a sense of intimacy.

La Escondida's kitchen is very long, with just enough extra space to hide the area where food is actually prepared, and where it is difficult to avoid a certain amount of culinary chaos. With this practical solution, all that shows is a well-ordered row of spices, and cooking utensils arranged purely for their visual effect.

Exterior walls, interior walls

«The challenge was to build a high-quality residence on a very narrow parcel, and it was met in such a way that the outdoor centers of attention, and the movement leading inside, have worked like sleight-of-hand to make the actual geographic limitations disappear.»

The pool is narrow, sensual, and far from rectilinear. Surrounded by palm trees, it daringly approaches the void that leads to the sea. To one side, flowers are allowed to express themselves fully in a roof garden. A series of concrete rectangles acts as an occasional sunscreen.

Beyond the patio is a staircase that leads to the guestrooms. «This is an idyllic place, in which privacy plays one of the most important roles.» The environments built here are all based on that primal goal.

Once you take the first step down to the guestrooms, the connection with the rest of the house vanishes: friends and hosts say goodbye to one another and forget that there are other living souls anywhere around. Each of the bedrooms has its own balcony with glass handrails – «so as not to place any visual obstacle between the house and the immensity of the ocean.»

The dimensions of the master bedroom, above the central edifice, reflect its importance in the domestic hierarchy, but its comforts don't surpass those of the other areas. The cupola above the room measures sixteen feet from the mosaic floor. The terrace is ample, full of flowers grown in window boxes, to hide the room from indiscreet glances. The bath does indeed announce its superiority rather loudly, and its ceiling is, again, what guides vision and motion. This room is so large that it gave Tapia the luxury of using a dark wood, without any complexes about how the tones affected the sense of space.

«Since I believe in the human soul, it is along the upper part of the walls, and not down on the floor, where my ideas are best expressed.»

In this house Próspero Tapia, loyal to his precedents, creates a new version of his architectural trademark, which demands that sensual forms take center stage.

CASA WEISS: A PERFECT SETTING FOR WONDERFUL PEOPLE

GEORGE AND CLAIRE WEISS
OWNERS

STEVEN HARRIS
ARCHITECT

LUCIEN REES-ROBERTS
INTERIOR DESIGN

TOM ZOOK AND ANTONIO ZANINOVIC
PROJECT TEAM

MARGIE RUDDICK
LANDSCAPE DESIGN

In formal terms, Casa Weiss is a house which responds to its particular environment. It is placed high in the hills of El Pedregal, a natural stone outcropping that overlooks the Pacific Ocean.

The home's reality goes beyond its location, though, and speaks with melodious eloquence. More than just an array of walls, it is an entire atmosphere that frames endless patterns, captivating anyone who lives or visits here.

And so the scene presents itself: a glass of white wine, a well-known tune «What a wonderful world», 'the hosts' welcoming smiles. The estate rises on a marvelous stage that might be embedded in nothingness, sustained only by the ocean's waves, in equilibrium with the salt breeze and the floating clouds.

Made for each other

George Weiss has been a very successful composer for a long time; a serene man, with calm intelligence evident in his face. Claire, his wife, is a woman who gently achieves her aims, with delicate gestures and a warm expression. The property cannot be described without describing them. George's music colors each space, and Claire's sensibility completes the picture.

The specialists responsible for the work say that two basic criteria determined the proposal: to create an exterior space that would protect the privacy of both the homeowners and their

56

neighbors, and to simultaneously frame the views, near and far, of the existing natural landscape, correlating natural elements with the architecture. «Thus, the building occupies the edges of the property, permitting the interior to remain open, with the original vegetation and rocks,» says Antonio Zaninovic.

There is no doubt that these criteria have been met, but the home's exquisite placement is not all there is to its charm. Simply saying that the landscaping preserved local plant-life falls short of describing the full effect: indeed, the work is so subtle that the gardens seem untouched by human hands.

The central patio is a slice of desert highlighted with tall plants and surrounded by selected elements in a range of sand-tones. It should be emphasized that the original rocks have not only been preserved, but ingeniously located: to serve now as a cornerstone, then as a wall; here as an ornament, there as a screen.

Earth, wind and... water

This architecture springs from within the earth, rising softly from the surface and molding itself to the land's natural shapes and silhouettes, as they appear inside and out, through its distinct areas.

Antonio Zaninovic pauses at the entrance to offer a few details: «The house is located high upon the property, and it starts by submerging itself in the terrain, for a moment losing any notion of the sea. But the ocean reappears gloriously, framed by the two main wings and the natural elements, when we arrive at the entry pavilion. The construction appears ethereal, mobile, in spite of being firmly attached to the top of a cliff.»

From that instant on, from that sense of place, magic blows through like a breeze and the mood becomes musical. Chords and silence are interwoven as they move along the barely-present walls.

It would be useless to list or number all the fine objects here. Everything is in its natural spot, as if it had been there forever. We see them; but on another more important plane, we feel them.

The home's principal grace is not in that which is built, but in what is left free. Its accomplishment lies in the creation of emptinesses, where the soul may breathe. The result takes on the shape of magic: total balance, design and landscape hand in hand.

Every space, every piece of furniture, and every accessory tells of the Weiss' aesthetic sensibilities. It is a collection of good taste, in every sense.

As in the narrow swimming pool, located within a rocky canyon that aligns itself first with the cliff, and from there, with the sea. It is a planned explosion, with freedom awaiting only a few yards ahead.

An expert's words

«At first impression, a sculptural form is suspended above a watery element, which seems to float between land-masses. This is how relationships are established between the different components that make up the whole: they flow from the concept of a cave to that of an airy viewing platform.»

Zaninovic adds that light and water are interpreted in several ways throughout the project: «Under a suspended dividing wall, a channel of water runs between the patio and the main rooms, directing reflected light towards the interior and acting as a skylight for a glass shower-stall on the lower level».

Glass cylinders inserted in the wall of the east wing capture small images from the landscape, as they assure privacy from future neighbors. At specific times of the year at dawn's first light, these crystalline elements project a pyrotechnic light show onto an interior wall. Catching and guiding the sunbeams, they invite them to be part of the house.

Looking in from the patio we recognize the most commanding form of all: a grand piano placed in the living room. All the rest of the room's furnishings submit themselves to its black-and-white formality, and everything takes place around this instrument, with the sea listening in attentively, a faithful audience.

«Technicalities»

In terms of logistics, one of the clients' main requirements was that the most frequently-used areas be on the same level. For this reason, the master bedroom, bathrooms, gym and TV room share a floor in the east wing. The west wing is composed of living room, dining room and kitchen. The guestrooms, each with its own recreation area, are found on the lower levels of both wings.

«The project was first imbued with a sense of place and then developed in response to the needs and customs of its very sophisticated inhabitants, with local materials and construction techniques used to their highest expressive possibilities.»

Nothing in Casa Weiss is accidental, everything about its presence here is clearly intentional. Its rooms defy description, but magnificently offer themselves to enjoyment.

CASA
Nido

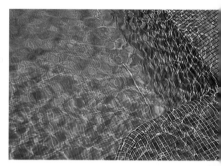

CASA NIDO:
AN AUTHENTIC MOUNTAIN DWELLING, WITH A VIEW OF THE SEA

WALTER AND VICTORIA SHAW
OWNERS

ARCHITECT RUBÉN ÁLVAREZ IBARRA
ARCHITECT ENRIQUE GARCÍA ÁLVAREZ
PROJECT

A house called «Nest» in Spanish, in the Sierra de Mar residential community; a perfect congruence between names and contexts. «Splashes of blue suffice for declaring its identity as a beach home, but the mountain demands its own treatment,» in the words of Enrique. Rubén and Enrique manage space, going beyond form to relate the two, and watch what the conjunction generates. Their professional goal consists of «placing things in order to see what there is to be seen...» This home was made as a function of human joyousness, not to reflect honors upon any one person.

It is a mountain home that looks out over the ocean: comfortable, practical, with a defined style, honest, simple in its delegation of space. Showing fine workmanship. What makes it distinct is its elevation: sitting on a mountain, looking down upon a deep tree-filled ravine.

The house is built according to the construction traditions of Puerto Vallarta, a place faithful to its geography, to its history as a country town which stretches down to the ocean. There it finds new inspiration, without detracting from its heritage.

«The sensations we have in the Vallarta houses of yesteryear are translated into this home, with adaptations relevant to the times in which it lives now, and the particular dynamics to be resolved within its walls. From there we address Casa Nido's spatial concepts, and then design the various environments: vestibule, central patio, wooden beams, gabled and tiled roof.» Casa Nido stands out in its surroundings, neither hiding itself

nor having any wish to dissemble. It belongs there, and its message is definite.

«What is required for good construction is what we use, and these materials have value as design elements.» The vestibule is boastfully Mexican. The entrance is framed by a thick wooden portico, supported by columns of quarry stone and riveted with metal. It watches over a pair of windows decorated with ironwork. The design statement is clear, without secret codes or double meanings.

Made to order

One particular merit of Casa Nido is that it was built to be sold: «It had to be easy for anyone to adapt to,» says Enrique. For a somewhat wider definition, the house maintains universal standards of quality, taste and emotional response: more of each, and better, because the architects took into account that the profile of its future inhabitants was undefined.

The requirements were sketchy if not ambiguous: four bedrooms in a Mexican home. They first located the bedrooms, always four no matter what, and then interpreted the Mexican style, Mexican everywhere, no matter what. Then the clay floor appeared, bordered with round pebbles, and the special Mexican quarry stone known as cantera – in stairways, pediments, details and finishing touches.

It is worth remarking that they achieved their goal, and that the house was sold even before construction began. It was a tight bargain made with the Shaws, to balance the budget and projected selling price. The only complaint the owners have had is that «their houseguests don't want to leave.»

*The ocean appearing within its panoramic view
is simply a geographic accident,
which embellishes but does not govern.*

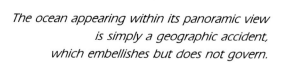

Never losing sight of tradition

Casa Nido leaves nothing to the imagination. On the contrary, it successfully manages to capture the best of the zone where it nestles. Having the mountain or the sea appear in every window are proofs of its limitless, but restrained, ambition.

The patio is an unequalled testament to tradition: boldly rectangular, it is reached by a corridor and flows into the main living room. To its right appears the mountain and to its left, the kitchen. In the center there is a fountain which if it lacks anything, it must be fragility: it is massively heavy, and yet produces trickling sounds that are barely audible.

What next? A friendly relationship between kitchen, living and dining rooms, terrace, patio-garden and hallways. Interesting contrasts abound, but nothing clashes. One detail: the quarry stone columns of the portico have now become mellow wooden rectangles, just by crossing the threshold. This is purely Mexican style, derived from different eras.

The kitchen doesn't go along with the U.S. system of meals: it maintains its distance from the dining room, preserving its independence – even when it is on hand for a typical U.S. barbecue. But then, it is always dressed up for company, with magnificent views anywhere you look. «Please let me wash the dishes!» guests might plead, just to enjoy the view. And after that chore, they may rest on the wide window ledge that looks back to the fountain and tree, and ahead to the mountain. In peace and tranquility, these sights compare admirably with any other panorama.

«The value of the house is that it remains true to Puerto Vallarta's architecture, which in its turn reaches to the village of San Sebastián del Oeste for inspiration. That's it.»

Here, as opposed to other tourist locations, there exist profound roots that cannot – should not – be ignored. Before becoming a destination for visitors from around the world, Puerto Vallarta was already a town, and already had its own personality.

Hierarchy

The importance of the living room – «because people congregate here, and here our most unforgettable moments happen» – is reflected in its ceiling. This feature obliged them «to place a bedroom at the same level as the dining room –good for market-

This property pays full attention to the Shaws' family dynamic, never abnegating its vocation as their vacation sanctuary. It possesses every attribute necessary to make it a true home.

ing to potential buyers of retirement age – then another above that, and another on top of the kitchen – there weren't many options.» The fourth bedroom that figured in the plans was in this case converted into a billiard room, studio and gym.

As for the characteristics of Álvarez and García (AG Arquitectos), Enrique notes that «we like to work the corners so that they have at least two orientations, two openings, and we like for the ceilings to have several gables – towers, separate volumes.»

The master bedroom on the first floor has a headboard wall that accomodates both the bed and the entrance to the bathroom. Its terrace is a continuation of the living room: and a direct route to the swimming pool.

It also has a typical balcony – with flowerpots and wrought iron – that looks out over the ravine, the hills, the lush green of the landscape. Lying in bed one may admire a mountain view to the right, and straight ahead, a view of the sea. Of course, gazing out over such splendor gives one a healthy dose of humility. The bath has no view of the waves, it is the mountains that seem almost to come in and pay a visit to the shower.

Another level

The staircase speaks of order, of pieces assembled in their natural niches, carefully, precisely. It opens on the upper hallway – a repeat of the hallway on the main level – to guide the wandering gaze into the guestroom. «It is the most modest room,» but its terrace offers a dramatic mountain view.

Across the way, the other bedroom is almost identical to the one below it, except that its ceiling is higher, and it has no terrace adjoining the pool. No matter: this room has much more mountain, and much more sea.

For the lower level – under the suite – the original plans envisioned a fourth bedroom. The Shaws decided that this was the ideal place for their gym and for Walter's studio, an ample area which would comfortably fit a living room set, a billiard table and a desk.

This is Casa Nido: set on a mountain, solid and sure of its personality – as long as it can also look out to the sea.

The mountain demands total attention,
and the house submissively obeys.
It looks toward the rocky crest,
though it also keeps an eye on the sea.

Casa del Risco

Casa del Risco:
A home with a privileged view, and no lack of comfort

ARCHITECT ÓSCAR ESPINOSA ALÍ MODAD
PROJECT

Officially, it's called Casa Cortés, but the project director likes to call it «Casa del Risco» (Cliff House). And no wonder: the sea roars, crashing violently on the rocks: it literally roars and crashes, not just figuratively. The surroundings are spectacular – enormous rock formations that are testaments to nature's patience as a sculptor – placed on a craggy peak, with the land below hurtling into the wild ocean. Casa del Risco is something of an understatement.

«With a property having such characteristics, including one of the best views of the Finisterra Arch, the question is 'where do I start?'; because when it comes down to it, all you would really need would be a roof to keep the sun out. Anything else is almost too much,» says Óscar Espinosa Alí Modad.

But he knows that they called him in as the architect to build, «which on occasion can actually mean 'change things'.» The fact is that the splendid panorama presented him with some difficulty: where might a house grow, on this rocky cliff?

Mediating ego and emotion
What he did, finally, was to integrate the building with the land forms, changing as little as possible. «The view is by far the most crucial factor, the reason why anyone chooses to live here. On the other hand, there is the weather, which forced other, structural, decisions: we aimed for proportions that would be comfortable for the inhabitants, forms that wouldn't be too risky, and plenty of safety factors.» Espinosa enjoys the house that came about as

The shapes here were a given; the land contained its own master plan. The house rose in accordance with the dictates of nature.

a result of his work, though he might have liked to see a more wide-open site for it. At the same time, he notes that the clients, who will live in the house, should have the privilege of making such choices: «it was they who decided this was the best site.» Respecting this principle meant playing with the view at every step of the building process.

Óscar quietly takes time to phrase a careful explanation of this particular principle. «After the creative stages, that time spent analyzing the site and being captivated with the setting, what one really becomes is an administrator of order. Casa del Risco is beautiful to look at from every angle. The rocks add to the beauty; the waves observe and enhance it.»

Espinosa refers to aesthetic emotion... «emotion and ego». For the client, assuredly, the aesthetic emotion is in looking at the sea, the sunset, the arch. He considers that for the architect, it is to be a mediator, and to enjoy the intensely creative process himself. After reflecting a bit more, he notes that any human work can always be improved upon, but that with the results of this particular project he feels content.

Angular stone

«The heart of the project is the tower,» a cylinder that constitutes the property's nerve center, and which «dictated how to work with the land.» Three levels rose from that natural form: on the first a bedroom, «the most dramatic one, for its proximity to the sea.» Here you feel the force of the tides, with a close-up view of the formidable rocks. On the second level – the social area – is located the family room, «which is also closely aligned with family dynamics». And in the highest part, the master bedroom takes advantage of a good portion of the 360-degree view, from within its own circular frame.

Three round spaces reflect the rhythm of the house, adhering to nature and departing from the straight lines of the rest of the house: they are discreetly decorated, and illuminated by offset but perfectly harmonious windows. Espinosa stresses that «the view from here and attendant sensations are very different from those perceived at the house's base,» and that the real work of the architect is just this: to elicit «diverse feelings in each area.»

House Tour

Before wandering through the house, it's worth noting that the décor consists of pieces chosen one by one, more to assemble a «collection» than to merely furnish the space. Entrance is via a small vestibule, a «brush-stroke that suggests and sums up what the house is about.» The palm ceiling was installed with the intention of making it informal – although it encloses the interiors in veritable altars to comfort – and to contrast with the sea below.

As if the blue of the waves were not enough, water also comes to life in the entranceway, which leads to the pool – which in its turn descends to the ocean.

The architect says that the topography determined the lines to follow, and his professional task was to strike a balance between the clients' wishes and those of the natural surroundings. Faithful and attentive to the patterns of the land, there is a guest bungalow to the right, with a direct seaward view. It has its own kitchenette, dining nook, terrace, dressing room and bath: privacy, intimacy, luxury. In fond accordance with a way of life that inclines to entertaining and celebrations, to the almost constant presence of friends, but which at the same time considers independence a primordial value.

Toward the other side is the house itself, with a pair of stair-steps in between. Living and dining rooms are brought together in one area; nearby is the TV room, raised a bit so it need not stop gazing at the horizon. The kitchen also appears, through the dining room. The tower rises strong and commanding, and calls forth all the energy and dynamism of the house. It has been here since the beginning.

Intimately communicating with its surroundings, the pool is a design solution tracing lines «which were already there, along with nature's 'instructions' for how it should relate to the home's interior.» Espinosa adds that this project «cried out for» a sense of infinity, effected by using the many shades of blue. It is not terribly large, but it is indeed impressive. «With its nearly 180-degree panorama, it is perhaps the other part of the house that has the greatest degree of drama.»

Curves abound, for reasons justified by comfort and ease. «They are evocative, and feel more like the lineaments of nature: they do not interrupt the precipitous feeling that surrounds the building.» Thus, the terrace steps down to join the swimming pool area. Two bedrooms share the upstairs with the master bedroom, and have no reason to covet any of its appurtenances, just its curves. As a whole, the structure breathes harmony, balance, tranquility. It does not deny the land, nor even impose its own coloration upon the site it occupies. The cliff has become a home, shaped with respect, and out of respect for the elements, built to safely shelter its new inhabitants.

The circular edifice is the house's main hub; the rest has been developed around it to promote harmonious communication.

CASA *Amore*

CASA AMORE:
A LIVING SPACE THAT KNOWS THE MEANING OF LIVING WELL

MOHAMED AND YOLANDA HADID
OWNERS

ARCHITECT JAIME BARBA
PROJECT

Strictly speaking, this home is not for guests: it lives for the Hadid family, for the three children whom it treats so well on their vacations, for their mother, a beautiful Dutch model who revels in it as much as the children do, and for their father, whose sojourns here are briefer but no less enjoyable.

The dwelling's name sprung from a woman's heart that had gone through some bitter moments – now happily overcome – which led its owner to decorate her home with much love. «Each object, each piece of furniture, was chosen with care, with feeling, for her children,» relates Josefa Bardales, the property's administrator, who knows just what she's talking about.

Yolanda Hadid's taste and attention colors every space: from the entrance pond, with its thatched roof providing some shade for the swans and with water enough for 150 fish to live there happily; to the barbecue patio next to the kitchen.

Blending cultural origins
It is a place to live, which becomes apparent right away: in the main entryway, enormous and narrow, which opens onto a wide living area where the owners' origins blend in the selection of furniture and accessories.

One's gaze moves freely through the space, lingering with curiosity upon the hallway's fountain – which gurgles merrily without interrupting the floor's horizontal line – and then upon the armchairs, tables full of family photographs, large oil portraits of the ladies of the house – which are works by Padilla. Further on you arrive at the terrace, the lawn, the pool, the trees from which hammocks hang, the sea: a domestic ocean, tranquil, bordered by golden sand. The dining room, unreservedly majestic, announces its purpose with a sturdy table of dark wood and the eleven chairs that surround it. Candleholders supported by beams, and fans made of tropical fronds, complete the scene.

The kitchen appears to be open to a social scene, and in fact it is, but a pair of aluminum doors subtly hide freezers, on the one hand – the everyday refrigerator is covered in the same wood as the shelving – and on the other, access to the barbecue patio. This is located to the rear, so that the chef can wield all sorts of culinary tools as he prepares a meal; the patio also has a bar, and various benches for the occasional cigarette. There, among discreet anterooms, is a room for whoever is in charge of putting on the music.

The main suite

«Bedroom», «chamber», or «suite»: none of these is a sufficiently stylish term for Mr. and Mrs. Hadid's domain. One end of the room is accessed from a small salon, with good natural illumination, containing Yolanda's desk, and there are doors to the dressing-rooms and the bath – an area which deserves its own description. Sinks recessed into antique commodes, a pair of wicker armchairs that receive fresh air from the private patio through wide windows, a majestic bathtub, and flowers in bloom everywhere.

A set of stairs invites us to venture up to another level. There above, a quintessential office, with mahogany-paneled walls, thick curtains and leather sofas provides the isolation that Mr. Hadid needs for uninterrupted work, even when he's far from his businesses. But working doesn't prevent him from being treated to a splendid view of the garden, the palm trees, the flowers, the sea...

The bedroom itself is very spacious, and it is opened up even more with a wall of mirrors. The bed is high and antique, and at its foot, inside a trunk from a much-earlier time, is a television system with a super-thin screen. Two chests function as bureaus, and the rest of the furniture bespeaks a taste for nobility, for authenticity, for cultural mixtures. The ceilings are necessarily high, but the warmth of the room's accessories counterbalance their dimensions.

Images of the family proliferate, pictures taken in happy, private, now-nostalgic moments. «She has a kind of mania for photographs,» Josefa Bardales, Yolanda's secretary, personal assistant, and friend, tells us.

The cellar

Under the main living space is the TV room, a corner from «The Thousand and One Nights», with comfortable seating cushions (and another 80 for backup), in different designs and textures, but all equally colorful.

To one side, the winecellar. A table at its center, temperature control, comfortable chairs. «Knowing how to live» seems to be the motto. An elevator from the kitchen opens just across from the doors, to convey anything that might be needed to these rooms.

This does not seem to be a vacation property,
but manages to look more like a year-round residence.
Every corner of the home
shows a propensity for permanence.

The hallway is a showplace for a collection of charro sombreros and riding saddles. «She is a horsewoman, and now so are her daughters.» Josefa also comments that Yolanda loves mariachi music: every time she holds a dinner at the house, she contracts a mariachi band to add to the festivities.

Neighboring areas

At the other side of the room is a door into a hallway. This leads to three bedrooms, the children's, with privileged views, terraces and gardens. Nearby is a magical realm, full of toys, which is also where the children take their summer classes, and a young teacher entertainingly reviews their lessons with them

Outside, parked very formally, stand a series of dune buggies, and further on, jet-skis. Above these bedrooms, another two were designed to welcome occasional visitors: one for adults, and one for children. These also belong fully to the landscape, and are denied nothing in the way of proportions, interior décor, or views. The thatch ceilings here are high, except in the quarters of the young Hadids.

«All the ambiences are separate, but related; there is plenty of privacy without any feeling of isolation,» says Josefa, who knows the house so well that she can walk through it «with her eyes closed.»

The decoration has been well thought out, to make any corner a welcoming spot: in passing, we come upon armchairs, chaise longues, chests displaying sculptures, and others holding mirrors.

Independent of the main passage, a long corridor bedecked with plants brings us to the guest house, with three bedrooms, a kitchen and sitting room. The common areas are outdoors; only the private ones are kept well-guarded.

Over there, a bit hidden, is the laundry and electrical power plant. Josefa is responsible for the house's upkeep, and supervises a team of thirteen people. Summer is the «high season» for the property, but during the rest of the year she stays on top of every detail so that the house can always be poised to receive the Hadid family.

The ceilings are very high,
and crowned with palapas that will not interfere
with the interior's formal decorative style.

CASA *Azul*

CASA AZUL:
UNSELFCONSCIOUSLY CHOOSING
FROM THE BEST TRADITIONS

DR. ANTHONY K. HEDLEY AND C.C. GOLDWATER
AKCC CORPORATION
OWNERS

ARCHITECT JACINTO ÁVALOS
ÁVALOS ARQUITECTOS ASOCIADOS
PROJECT AND CONSTRUCTION

This home has taken advantage of all its limitations, integrating each to serve the project. Thus the entryway acquired its role of a path leading to the main door: not only did Jacinto Ávalos decide to do away with sidewalks, but he appropriated the existing ones into his plan.

Casa Azul (Blue House) sits on a lot whose boundaries force it to rise to the challenge of seeming more ample than it is, «by allowing light to take over and create a sense of liberation, of infinity.» Jacinto Ávalos considers that the challenge was met, and the owners share his opinion. The architect also notes that by using colors he was able «to assimilate the building into the visual strip that represents sea, horizon, and sky».

All in all, the house achieves the ideal balance between formal architecture, landscape and interiors. There is a harmony that can be felt whether one is comfortably seated in any armchair, or randomly selecting a terrace from which to lean out and appreciate the view.

Jacinto is convinced that in his profession some of the best architectural ideas have the additional quality of bearing unanticipated «housewarming» gifts with them. «It's incredible, the way the light dances about at certain times of the day, hopping from one wall to another, and then charging into the house itself.» The opulence of Avalos' architecture surely lies in the fluidity and the many subtle shadings of his spaces.

It is easy to detect this characteristic in his work; all we have to do is to see one of his homes and the ways its inhabitants enjoy it, or to discover for ourselves the permanent sense of wellbeing there is in every angle, stance and activity. Jacinto Ávalos is rigorous in all that he does, and in Casa Azul one recognizes his purpose and his strength. In his line of work, there are no accidents.

The estate
The clients play a vital role in the final outcome of the project, their contribution enriching the architect's.

The building lot had its own difficulties: in terms of topography it was elevated, but it was also surrounded by a series of houses which restricted its ocean view. On the other hand, family dynamics required that rooms be a certain distance from one another. Given these challenges, the house was built on four levels. At street level, there is a parking area, the second level holds bedrooms and guest quarters, the third has become a social area, and the fourth accomodates both the master suite and another guestroom.

«As far as was possible, I gave each space its own view.» Not only that, but Jacinto created light-filled areas for enjoying moments and events: inviting shade or blazing sun, or even a bit of both, in just the right combination for a quintessentially unhurried afternoon.

The entryway
The handling of entrances is important to Jacinto. «This is the first impression, what distinguishes the experience of arriving at a home, and in each of my projects I have taken an interest in creating this initial impact.» So in this patio, built upon a model that has existed for centuries or even milennia, we find a central fountain, trees all around providing a play of light and shadow, adobe brick walls for the necessary windbreak, a proportionate amount of landscaping, a bench that is truly serviceable and not just an aesthetic touch. Quietly faithful to Ávalos approach, this is a typical welcome to a Mexican home, offered by timeless

It is Mexican, and blue: open, and functional.
It reinterprets spatial solutions to turn them
into zones of fresh air and affability.

household gods. There is the temptation to stop right here: but something, inexplicably seductive, calls to us from inside. In Casa Azul, unlike some of Jacinto's other homes, the view is on the same side of the property as the entryway, and though it opens into the public thoroughfare, it also remains introverted.

The selection of design elements is minimal, but nevertheless stands out as soon as we ascend the first step from the street. Without any preamble, we notice that the house has a visual cadence all its own. Not yet having seeing anything of the house or of its neighbors, visitors are given time to prepare themselves for the experiences that await them. Once past the freshness of first glances, we enter the formal doorway and what appears is a kind of spiral that seems to simultaneously stretch out and curl into itself, as in a womb. Its shape suggests hallways running between walls that are not enclosed, but allow light to penetrate. The parlor and dining room are separated by one such wall, which elegantly serves to differentiate the two areas.

The living room is the first to call attention to itself. It has an adobe wall with delicate mortarwork that has been inset with small pebbles. An enormous painting hangs upon this wall, and the juxtaposed images, their shades evoking motion, are bathed in graduated sunlight.

Privacy

Part of the project's premise is that this should be a comfortable home, with spaces well interrelated and organized, and in perfect agreement with the land.

Up above is the master bedroom. Its importance is felt in its advantageous view and, more than anything, the garden that goes with it: a veritable orchard of exultant green. Its commanding presence makes a strong argument for a beach house set in Baja California's desert. The bedroom shares the limelight with a sitting room and a large bath. From a given point in the room, you can catch a glimpse of the breaking waves on one side, with fruit-laden branches on the other.

Before going downstairs we enjoy a luminous visual finale, thanks to a skylight that has been «tossed fifteen feet into the air» to take charge of allowing the sun in, and circulating the breeze. Once on the lower level, the bedrooms open up to show the perfect amount of privacy, of unostentatious luxury, of custom-designed views – not of the sea, but of an extravagantly secluded world.

The entrance patio calls attention to all that follows, but without offering too many clues. Inside, doors open onto architectural feats that exceed our expectations.

VILLA CELESTE: ORGANIC FORMS RAISED TO SENSUAL HEIGHTS

PROTIP
CONSTRUCTION

ARCHITECT PRÓSPERO TAPIA
PROJECT

CYNTHIA AND ALEJANDRA TAPIA
INTERIOR ARCHITECTURE DESIGN

The site occupied by this house is extraordinary. It is perched on the top of a dune, looking down on a wide panorama, with sand caressing its feet. The rocky landscape here takes on the role of a formal sculptural element, reflecting the light whose direction and shadows change every minute; a fortuitous obstacle that keeps the sea at bay. Here the wind is no euphemism, it is a wild roaring that forces serious technical considerations.

According to Prospero «we just integrated the construction with the largest stone.» The result is a house that is also nourished by the «largest star», and enjoys the sun's light and shadows; a formal, forceful, organic, and at the same time capricious abode.

In Tapia's projects there is a constant desire to break with the conventional, the strictly formal. Villa Celeste is one more demonstration of the peculiar way he first conceives of spaces, and later brings them to life.

The façades, as is palpably shown, mimic nature; their fluidity emulates what already exists; something unrestrained, independent, undulating. Or as Próspero would put it, «the hills are not linear»: textures and colors descend to be reproduced in the house, and hill-inspired images are brought into its hallways and humblest corners.

Perplexity

From the entrance everything tells us that surprise awaits us here, that it is going to jump out before we can blink an eye. This is no false promise: the entry fountain, fence and patio are themselves just the house winking disarmingly at visitors, to take them off guard.

A large rock is the property's most important ornament, unless you count its wonderful view and its privileged setting.

Pausing at the door, we see water flowing silently along a series of colored moldings. We don't know just where the liquid originates, nor where it might wind up.

Between the fenced perimeter and the house, there is an outdoor gallery, full of palm trees, of hand-wrought stars, of barely-discovered spaces. It is a rich transition from the harshness of the street, through the carports, and into the sensual interior. A two-way area that screens entrances and exits, and prepares us for what comes next.

«When its job is done and the sun takes its leave, what starts up here is a play of tri-colored lights, located in the bases of the treetrunks and tucked inside the metal stars.»

And there, in the middle of «the gallery of movable soffits and architraves», an area without apparent explanation but full of movement, appears the solid principal doorway.

The owner is as responsible as Tapia for the final version of Villa Celeste, since he gave the architect *carte blanche* to put his ideas into effect, over twenty months.

Ample and unhampered

A pair of wooden panels open into the living room; enormous in width and height. Rooms are differentiated with the use of textures, wall colors, ceiling tracks. To the left, the kitchen; at the center, the dining room; to the right, a generous living room. Everything is guarded by strong doors that can also instantly disappear.

Somewhat hidden away, not quite willing to come out in public, is an office-library-tv room.

Interior areas are completely in congruence
with the splendid exterior, and are just as spacious
and capricious as the natural context.

Tapia does not subject himself to established forms:
for him, the creative process is a constant playful exercise,
and the lively results show in the homes he designs.

The walls' patina is the result of several superimposed tones, applied independently in the manner of the Impressionists, who mixed colors just until they had a palette that they could use to lightly layer one atop another, unblended.

Outside, on the terrace, more confirmation that this is one of Próspero Tapia's designs – governed by playful irreverence, going on the principle of inventing new building methods, individualizing structures. His imagination stops at nothing, quite the contrary: his ideas confidently convert themselves into tangible form, depth and dimension.

The location of the pool transforms it into a magic carpet of water, looking like the white-capped sea, with delicate interwoven tones – all requiring special equipment to keep it from succumbing to the merciless winds.

Tapia carries organic forms to the point of sensuality – he adapts freely, and what best meet his objectives, such as reproducing the rolling forms of the landscape, are traditional, classic, or contemporary materials.

The bedrooms

A corridor that forces concrete to meander, stretching in some places and swelling in others, leads to the master bedroom, whose vaulted ceiling is also irregularly-formed. It rambles through an extraordinary version of a nautilus – greatly resembling the maternal womb, as seen from within – which incidentally hides the grill of the air conditioner.

The furniture provides contrast, now and then making a futile attempt to tone down all the structure's divertissements.

For Tapia right angles are not obligatory; several walls prefer to let themselves go, and copy the surrounding landscape. The rocks remain where they've been for many, many years, and in some cases their venerable forms have been specially reproduced to be placed in locations where no stone originally stood.

Another corridor, that also agrees with the architect's whims, rises organically to face the upper-level entrance. One door leads to another, and yet another. Wooden doors with carved motifs, all different and all conscientiously orienting the fortunate inhabitants to this space adorned with artistry.

Essentially, Villa Celeste has appropriated one of Los Cabos' best sites for itself, and moved into it with assurance, irrepressibly accented by a spirit of fun.

The dunes made room for the building to be constructed on a gentle rise, surrounded by a sensual landscape. The walls of the house follow the sand's visual rhythms.

CASA CANELA:
PRACTICAL, ECONOMICAL, WITHOUT EMBELLISHMENTS OR EXTRAS

THOMAS AND JOAN MONAHAN
OWNERS

16/16 ARQUITECTOS
DESIGN

ARCHITECT JAIME OCHOA QUIÑÓNEZ
ARCHITECT NICOLÁS OROZCO DÍAZ
ARCHITECT SERGIO RIESTRA HERNÁNDEZ
GRUPO CONSTRUCTOR GKOOR
CONSTRUCTION

Its lines rise cleanly, and even the sightless walls take note of the structure's candid personality. The name it bears, «Cinnamon House» or Casa Canela, has everything to do with color.

«This shade was taken from the bark of the *papelillo* – a typical tree of the region – with the intention of losing the structural mass amidst the surrounding vegetation,» Jaime Ochoa tells us. The property is large – well over an acre – and was selected after it was seen from the beach. It starts at the street and ends on a cliff top, with stairs leading down to the waves, and a stone-incrusted platform for storing ocean kayaks.

The front door opens upon terrain that seems so wild that it nearly obscures the pavement that takes us to an entrance patio, where there rests a stone that acts as a sometime-fountain. «I sat on this stone when I came to analyze the space and imagine the project.» Now water flows through the natural channels it already had, and the installation contrasts with the pure geometry of the forms nearby.

The vestibule has a window in its far wall, and doors to each side. Their purpose, first, is to open onto glimpses of the landscape, just subtle brush-strokes to indicate the whole masterwork of nature which explodes outside. Secondly, of course, they offer cross-ventilation, and refreshing coolness.

The living room is simple, free-spirited and dedicated to providing refuge: it might be a sunken indoor patio, or a protective stronghold. Put succinctly, high ceilings and neutral furnishings.

Respect for the existing trees was paramount,
and the home's façades were built
in a spirit of allowing an unimpeded view.

«The house can close itself off from the world by means of shutters, as well as sliding windows and doors.»

Next comes the terrace – expansive – and then the garden. The former uses South American *guayabillo* wood in a structure that protects sunbathers from too much sun, and softens the light in general. «The idea is to give the feeling of a tropical palapa, without resorting to stereotypes.» A lawn adds to the verdant area which is regularly used and enlivened by members of the household.

In the distance a tanning area is installed, shaped like a ship's bow that appears on the cliff; a slightly elevated platform without retaining walls or other interfering structures.

Subtly forceful

«Thomas and Joan's primary wish for the property was that it should demand almost zero maintenance,» and from there a selection was made of materials especially suited to the climate and the salty breezes. Teak was used for the exterior window frames and some of the garden furniture; with the sun's help, it takes on earthen tones, grays with silvery streaks, and needs no varnishing or oiling. Polished concrete covers the floors in sand-tones; the same surface is painted white in the bathrooms. The interiors reflect the intention to keep things simple, with indirect lighting shining on just a few carefully-selected decorative objects.

*Teak, polished cement, furniture selected
to be functional and unobtrusive;
precision and subtlety for a home
that requires virtually no maintenance.*

«We left out everything that wasn't necessary,» says Jaime. A concise phrase that demonstrates a masculine attitude, one which also imbues the building design and is translated into a clearcut visual dialogue, where no one needs to dig for meaning or mixed messages.

«This is a theater set for highlighting nature's accomplishments, with the land itself having more lines to deliver, and the house yielding center stage.»

The swimming pool contains an island with three trees: it was unthinkable to move them, so they were integrated in the plan. Its boundaries imitate the surrounding forms, as do its colors.

Color and respect

«The Monahans have the same concern that we do for nature, and we were fortunate to share the same degree of respect for environmental preservation.»

The garden becomes part of the ravine, sitting right in the middle of it. «We left the property just the way it was, not even changing drainage or runoff patterns. In fact, this cleft in the land was the departure point for the development of the project.»

The house is divided in three: an apartment for the owners, with their bedroom, kitchen, carports - and the possibility of isolating themselves, or even closing off the rest of the house; the social area with a suite on the upper level; and three bedrooms with a tv room in the third section.

Halfway upstairs is Mr. Monahan's office; another flight and you pass through a vestibule to the master bedroom. This contains a full sitting room - it fits three 3-cushion sofas, as well as generous tables. Bath, terrace, privacy. Shutters are commonly used in Casa Canela: to manage wind, sun, and time alone.

The rest... there, across the way. Pragmatism at any cost, with no place for meddling or misinterpreting.

The other bedrooms are more of the same, not competing in grandness with the master suite but not receiving any less respectful treatment, either. Their location is thoughtfully designed as an ode to privacy, for all. Above, on what would be the rooftop garden or service area, there is an outlook with a 360-degree panoramic view: hills, ocean, seashore all fit into the visual field.

Joie de vivre lives and breathes within these walls, with no formalities. Creating wellbeing through ambience, textures and sensations is the only extravagance. This is part of an ecosystem that gets involved spatially: connection, circulation, existential flow.

The garden frames spatial concepts that developed
without complications nor affectations.
Interiors and exteriors commune
though shared premises, borne of respect.

VILLA
La Roca

Villa La Roca:
The details speak of moderation – the landscape, of daring

CHARLES AND SUSIE MORGAN
OWNERS

ENGINEER JORGE CARRERA T.
ARCHITECT ANTONIO CARRERA T.
MCA
PROJECT AND CONSTRUCTION

It is very difficult to appreciate it from a single vantage point. There is not only the height upon which this house is set, but the rocks below, those formations which have such a definite Los Cabos personality, such precise colorations and distinctive volumes.

One of the property's most striking virtues is the scenery: La Roca, «the Rock», enjoys a panoramic view of over 200 degrees, allowing one to truly see the landmark called Finisterra, «Land's End».

«In the beginning, the original idea was that the house would rise upon the platform that we cut into the mountain; little by little it was moved downward until it fit into our projected design of a road above and one below, with six levels in between,» recounts Jorge Carrera. When the work-in-progress was viewed without any subtle details or picturesque touches added, it appeared massive and heavy, and the architects decided to reinforce that sense of weight: quarry stone columns, balustrades and pediments lend serious solidity. But at the same time, so that it would not be so huge as to overshadow other structures, they scaled the building, in both senses: adjusting its size to, and stepping it evenly within, the cliff. It is majestic, and seems to belong to a member of the «landed gentry» – which is not far from reality, full as it is of antiques and collectibles.

Necessary force

Technical difficulties – such as how to completely transform a granite mountain – lengthened the process to two years, Jorge Carrera tells us, «because we also began on two fronts, at both upper and lower street levels.» He adds some details: «The structure of the house remains bound to the land in such a way that even where one part might have problems, the rest would not be affected; it functions as if it is on edge, though it is actually not.» Nor does it have a floorplan which flows and overlaps; each of its six storeys emanates its own feeling of obdurately

standing on its own firm ground. Here lives a family, and a valuable collection of antiques and artworks.

«Dramatic» is the exact word to denote the land from which Villa La Roca rises. Carrera's work could fall under the heading of «security»; walls anchored by tradition, by conserving the past. An exceptional way of integrating a home into terrain that has little to do with humans, placed on – or in – a cliff, facing the open Pacific Ocean and with sensual and cerebral repercussions from the sea.

Random data

The view is everywhere: that is to say, wherever one's glance alights, it is rewarded with delight...even in the garage. Those windows without seascapes, in the entrance hall facing the street, have leaded panes which gorgeously distort shapes, while still permitting light to pass through. The result: myriad shades of green, in continual motion.

The house's flooring is polished travertine marble edged with flagstone. Dark woods for the exterior, light for the interior. The doors, in line with the home's forcefulness, are four inches thick.

A computer has the job of controlling the lighting, faithfully responding to the owners' preferences at the touch of a small button; pre-programmed to set any needed light levels into play.

Congruence

The circular vestibule is topped, far up above, by a cupola. The main nave is very tall; 26 feet, ending at an interior balcony. There is also a hallway on the top storey which looks out over the living room, and in passing, over the wide sea: through a series of windows with double arches and columns.

The dining room is serious, with heavy ceiling beams and moldings. Set in its own space, it looks out onto the street, but has little relation to it. It is elevated somewhat so that the view reaches it, unobstructed, via the living room.

The family area is distinguished by a border of three steps, among many other details. It encompasses the kitchen and a hidden TV room. It is frank and unequivocal about its purpose, boasting a ceramic railing and handmade wooden doors.

On that level we find the library, the office and the master bedroom, with its bath and dressing rooms: more than 16,000 square feet clearly designated as the owners' realm. The suite's

The decoration is very formal, in bold contrast with the site the home occupies: its stability serves as an anchor for the building's daring location.

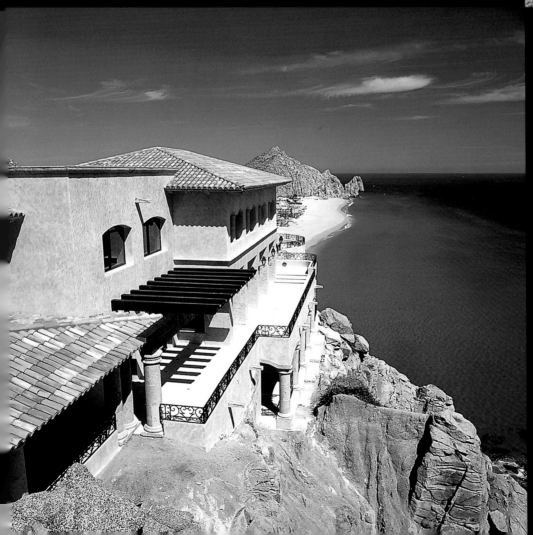

terrace is completely suspended over the edge, its ultimate test being a round of tempered glass 5 feet in diameter and 3/4 inch thick that is set into the floor and allows one a view of the chasm, the sea and rocks below. From there one can also truly appreciate the incisions that were made in the mountain for «inserting» the house.

This zone has the ability to isolate itself from the rest, by means of screens that give the owners their own «manageable» area.

The other five bedrooms are humbler – if that is a word to describe any part of this house – and because of structural levels, their views have a less panoramic quality.

Levels of moderation

The décor represents a different approach: a house as substantial as the rock it scales, in a completely clear, open and distant landscape, has decided to adorn itself with antiques. It seems to deny its audacious location by means of warm and hospitable rooms and heavy period furniture, to counterbalance the boldness of its site.

An attempt to commune with the landscape's exuberance, in its own language; forceful, but just as eloquent.

One floor below, there is a wide terrace, pool, jacuzzi and barbecue. An area slightly elevated above the rest becomes the perfect home for the telescope which, like the lighting system, is electronic. «It sets its sights on Venus and brings it into view,» says Carrera. And without special lenses one can see the Cerro Colorado volcano, San José del Cabo and the Pacific Ocean.

Gym, steam room, sauna, nothing is lacking. A hi-tech conference room, with complete kitchen. The house also has a tower which contains its staircase and elevator.

Otherworldly shapes and materials, from another era, are placed in a novel location: simply an archway and some railings facing the sea, but at such a stunning height above the waves that they are thoroughly unexpected.

So high in the air and yet so solid – an apparent contradiction, a play of paradoxes.

The mountain was trimmed to accommodate the six solidly-built levels of a house which can neither hide itself nor blend in, because of its sheer size.

CASA *Clark*

CASA CLARK:
IT SEEMS LIKE ONLY YESTERDAY, THOUGH IT'S BEEN TEN YEARS

ARCHITECT JACINTO ÁVALOS
ÁVALOS ARQUITECTOS ASOCIADOS
PROJECT AND CONSTRUCTION

«Each time I have the opportunity to visit, this house surprises me, and I still get pleasure from it. Also, a lot of satisfaction, knowing how the owners enjoy it. I did good work: it's the same house we built ten years ago with no modifications, and it still shows no signs of age. No damage from the humidity, no cracks in the walls,» Jacinto Ávalos comments calmly, pausing in his speech as he looks around. If Casa Clark were a woman, one could say that she hadn't even developed any wrinkles, after ten years.

The property looks very large, but it isn't. Viewing it from various angles, what stands out are its cupolas, with their glimpses of color. While it might seem to occupy more than 3000 square feet, it barely measures half that – which is sufficient space for its original purpose. Jacinto recalls the days when he was designing the project: «I was walking around with a lot of built-up pressure, a whole range of ideas, of goals for what I might accomplish in a house on a parcel like this one.» The result speaks for itself: a home that works on an aesthetic level as well as a utilitarian one.

A question of ethics

Ávalos emphasizes that honesty is important in establishing the site for a house, in building it with respect for the land and the environment. He assures us that he frequently stops by to «see» – in his mind's eye, at least – all the projects that he has developed throughout his life as an architect. Even when he is not physically in front of a house he's designed, he can precisely locate any errors: «whether of omission or comission; I know where it hurts, and it does hurt.» What he's talking about is a question of ethics.

For him, this particular house is exceptional, as it was a project where the client and the architect were fully attuned to one another.

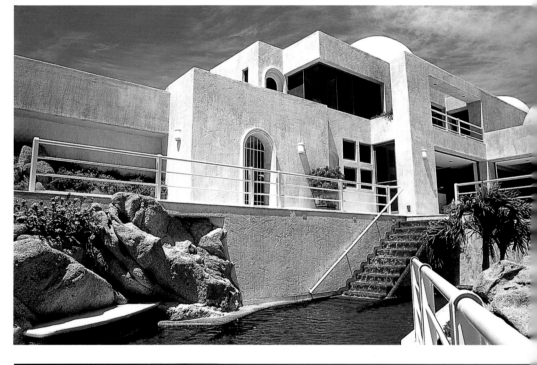

What stand out are five round cupolas, and the clean lines of its façades. Casa Clark has already become a part of the Los Cabos landscape.

Lighthearted nostalgia

The original paint is still on the walls. The fountains are still in good voice, and the roof gardens are still blooming.

The rooms are simple and spare, the bathrooms continue their playful game of up-and-down, built as they are on staggered levels so as not to lose a moment in seeking the view.

When Jacinto talks about the dimensions of the five bedrooms he notes that, «as far as sizes go, people have an idea that doesn't really have anything to do with necessity, it seems to be a bit more about yearning to build a huge monument to themselves.» He remembers the budget for this project, and figures that his intuition about just where to invest his resources back then was correct. «They have the minimum here, not bordering on insufficiency, but just exactly enough,» 11.5 x 11.5 feet, for example, in the room we're in. «This house is the prototype for a series of concepts that were valid at the time, and they still are.» A spherical cupola rises over every room, with a rim of small glass windows where it joins the wall. At night, exterior lamps illuminate the property; during the day, skylights bring sun to the interiors. The closets are integrated into the rooms, and there are windowseats under the windows, inside and out; in neither case is any floorspace lost from the living areas.

News from long ago

Jacinto started work on Casa Clark with what has become one of his characteristic approaches: arrangements of rounded rocks, or gardens, for the otherwise unused spaces of the flat rooftops. He's pleased to have seen that what was then a real innovation in his work has now been imitated in other building projects throughout the area. Nor does he pass up the chance to highlight the fact that «the rooms under the roof-gardens, ten years later, have had no trouble with dampness.» The interior environment has no superfluous elements, nothing to distract the eye, no bombardment of unnecessary information. «The house celebrates the view, the rocky terrain,» he says, reminding us that the house is situated in balance with the real majesty of the landscape. He is not a minimalist, but applies some of the principles of that school of thought, and abstains from using anything that is not required. Just as he is a man of few words, never losing himself in grandiloquent speeches.

The sun travels through the property, sometimes with total abandon, more often with a sense of moderation. Patios, terraces and gardens are open to its rays, and are dazed in varying degrees by their brightness.

Not only is the house a success architecturally, but nothing has been added in the way of decorative elements since the day the owners first arrived to occupy it; actually, Jacinto would have liked it better if the space hadn't been left untouched quite so definitively. «I don't want to see it stuffed with objects, but maybe a few sculptures, an interesting piece or two, some new furniture for the social areas.»

Just arrived

From the outside, looking up for example at Casa Clark's cupolas, we also appreciate Jacinto's work. The architecture calls for an even more careful examination – if that is the word – when we come upon something small, like the gentle sounds of the filters that he uses to bring moving water into his projects. For him the sound of the sea is not enough of an acoustical baffle: there are still areas in a house that are vulnerable to noise pollution from the street or neighboring properties. «Water is always present in my buildings, as a generator of sound, a «music-maker» might even be the more correct term, that helps drown out the noises from outside, and helps to relieve any static spaces. The idea is to desensitize the inhabitants to any distractions from the world beyond their own home.

On the same subject, something is about to change the property's physiognomy – an imposing neighbor. The new presence is a fact of life, as is the change in the *milieu*. Although the affected terrace still commands a view that runs between formidable rocks down to the sea, «because we built it anticipating that there might one day next-door neighbors» – there is still a sense of intrusion. What will alleviate the sensation of being watched, unknown during the ten years of almost absolute privacy, is the plant-life around the house.

Luckily, adds Jacinto, «the owner bought the land across from the future construction, and will expand Casa Clark in that direction: with another pool, a gameroom, a master suite, and more views.»

Casa Clark is a an example of guessing right when it comes to design solutions: set on a good piece of ground, it is a house that both owner and creator view with satisfaction. It has already become a part of the natural appearance of this Baja California beach.

Where it faces the street, the home is almost hermetically sealed, with no desire to participate in external activity. But then it throws caution to the winds, and its rooms spread out to receive the ocean breezes.

VILLA *Cathy*

VILLA CATHY:
A FEMININE HOUSE, CHANGING
FROM ONE MINUTE TO THE NEXT

CATHERINE ANN DOLLY WEBER KOHLER
OWNER

ARCHITECT GUSTAVO ORTIZ DE ZÁRATE
REALIZATION AND CONSTRUCTION

Las Clavellinas, the Spanish word for garden pinks, is the name of the beach which the house overlooks, from its clifftop site. Cathy, its Swiss owner, is a lover of Mexico, of Mexico's many colors, its vegetation, its seashores. Her great dream was to create something here which would be precisely like the home she now has. She began by talking over her desires with her sister Gaby, and Gaby's husband Ivanhoe Cruz Echeverría, who is also Gustavo's brother. «We laid everything on the table, and exchanged a lot of opinions. From there we came up with a plan of action, and a kind of sketch on paper of how the house would evolve.»

«As the architect, I concentrated upon capturing Cathy's teeming ideas in a way that could be built, adapting them to the land so that they could become walls, interior vignettes, views,» Gustavo tells us.

Productive dialogue

Ortiz de Zárate clearly remembers the process: «We spent hours deliberating. We were dealing with a property of almost twenty-five acres in co-ownership with 11 other residents.» The rules for building on this estate are clear; there are restrictions on the size of the floor plan, but none on the house's height as long as the roof is done in palapa style.

Cathy's dream took shape, «meeting all the architectural, structural and logistical challenges»; with respect and attention to the setting in its wild state. The adventure took three years and still is not finished.

The land had a 45-degree slope. «The house as such is ready, but there's a world of work remaining to be done on the exteriors – final touches, bringing landscape architecture into what is now

sheerly natural terrain, which is of course beautiful but still needs some color, some roads, lights and sound. There are many ideas still on the drawing board.»

In the middle of the jungle, the property has all its utilities, with their installations designed to be out of sight. The jungle continues along its way, calmly producing its wild cacophony of thousands of crabs, birds and plants, but also with civilized touches in its innermost reaches.

«The basic concept for the work grew from assimilating the talks with Gaby, Cathy and my brother.» These thoughts were embodied in four circles arranged around a central one. Each of the four encompassed an area that was laid out in relation to a circular hallway, and the center circle remained open. The largest of the circumferences correspond to the living room, dining room and kitchen; the rest accommodate the bedrooms, with their baths and terraces.

All was developed according to fairly uncommon themes, in frank and open «anti-urbanization». «It's not a totally rustic setting, but it aims to combine preexisting elements with innovative ideas.»

Personality

Villa Cathy bears its essential femininity proudly: it communes with its surroundings, it is a dreamer. It was neither completely governed by formal architectural canons, nor did it depart completely from them: not submitting itself to any standard, nor obeying the rules, yet it benefitted from experience. It only accepted those additions that were required in order for it to function as a real home, and which honored its goal of functioning with the topography.

Nevertheless, the place where the house has come to live is so lovely that the structure can delicately accept its pride of place without wanting to call attention to itself – although it is not totally self-effacing. Its palm roofs appear to be magical characters standing tall amidst the dense surrounding vegetation. This is the

Circles come together and open up, each
with a particular function to perform, each containing
a specific atmosphere. Outside, the jungle
continues along its way, always a faithful companion.

sort of whimsicality a beautiful woman typifies. The house insists that it tries to stay on the best terms with, and accommodate itself to, the surroundings, and it largely manages to do so. But it is impossible for us to take in its own beauty with just a glance, and just as impossible to avoid seeing it. Arrogant humility, a common female attitude.

Interiors

The entrance is 100% organic, allied with the contours of the land, adorned with stones in a subtly filigreed design.

Along with the circular bedrooms, the house has two independent bungalows – if such a word can be used for such private sanctuaries. Each has a kitchenette, terrace, bath and service area. They were built according to regional construction methods, «they are *pajareques* which are made by covering local *guayabillo* wood with stucco – which in this case is left natural on the exterior walls. Interior walls are covered with prefabricated material.»

During the final stage, artist Efraín Melendez was invited to add touches of color and texture to the work. As Gustavo tells it, Efraín provided a great service in enhancing the space. «The colors of the walls are his – yellows, purples –, the placement of the individual tiles, the carved cantera headboards, in all the spaces where such decorations appear.»

Details

There is a fountain, with logs that cause the water to jump, play, murmur a thousand drowsy sounds, splash through the tranquility and sing in unison with the ocean's eternal surf-sounds.

The entire house is a breathing entity which changes with each cloud that floats in front of the sun, each passing moment. On occasion it is a woman dressed to go out in evening clothes – though it cares nothing for exclusive fashions – but at other times, it remains comfortable, nearly nude, and simply relaxes.

The house demands strict maintenance, to put it mildly: «If you don't take care of it constantly, nature comes in and eats it up. When there are no people around, the *tejones* or coatimundis stroll through the house at will: they open the refrigerator, eat what they find, even stick their paws into the stove and the microwave. They're always the first ones to arrive.»

With no neighbors, it is only observed by the profuse vegetation that surrounds it. It is not luxurious, just filled with the magic of occupying a prominent height that is completely open to the Pacific.

El Encanto
de la Laguna

El Encanto de la Laguna: Just the beginning of a thriving neighborhood

Darío Antón / CDG
DEVELOPER

Sandy Espinet
INTERIOR DESIGN

This is a placid home, with nothing pretentious about it. In its desert-dominated setting, it calls forth a special joyfulness, interwoven with tranquility.

The property forms part of a complex of forty-two homes that will, in time, be built upon 42 acres of land. In the silence of its landscape, so removed from any human hustle and bustle, it could never, even with those 41 future neighbors, be called part of a housing subdivision.

This is not a place to visit for just a few days between other destinations, nor is it just a «vacation home». It is a serious abode, although it will most probably be the third or fourth one that the owners possess.

A quarry stone fountain offers the first hint of the Mexican flavor to be found within. The sturdy wooden door allows one to do no more than guess at the sea which lies beyond.

Once inside, we find a hallway crowned by a cupola of what appears to be brickwork. Strong pillars of quarry stone support the roof, a high stair-step serves as a occasional bench, and when night falls a candelabra provides illumination.

The large living room, bedecked in formal furniture and refreshed with woven wicker fans, flows out toward the sea.

Two giant bird-of-paradise plants preside over the scene. «They take years to bloom, but their size, colors and forms make the wait worthwhile,» Sandy tells us, proud of what she's

It is part of a group of homes, but enjoys a favored location: simultaneously at the edge of the sea and in the middle of the desert. It doesn't seem to be a vacation house, but a place to live one's entire life.

145

accomplished. Ultimately, it is she that has given personality to this house, which was turned over to her with the barest minimum of features needed to make it a home.

Feminine touch

The décor deserves special mention. It is comfortable without looking informal, elegant with neither strictness nor restrictions. It never forgets that it embellishes a property by the ocean, but neither does it abandon its intent to be lived in, for more than just a brief holiday.

Sandy is the person responsible for the interior design, and here the practice of her profession seemed to be especially challenging, because the house had no owner yet: «I had to create an atmosphere that would attract anyone.» The developers gave her a few clues: California and Mexico. The design of both regions should be taken into account, and Sandy's job was to make sure that the mixture of the two presented no strident visual leaps.

The interior design includes antiques, without blushing at such daring. There are wardrobes, tables, chunks of carved wood to form galleys, small boxes inlaid with ivory, candelabra and framed art. Also, Sandy has a weakness for mirrors and she managed – almost without realizing it – to select ones that were framed in diverse materials, sizes and shapes. They glisten everywhere, defending their bright vocation even when surrounding elements compete for attention.

Neutral tones were used for the large furniture, with touches of blue scattered here and there to emulate the natural shades outside: specifically, the colors of the sea. The ocean is an earnest presence, not murmuring but roaring, omnipresent not simply as landscape but as stark, unsubtle reality.

Some walls are painted with floral motifs, and Mexican influences sparkle everywhere. Some handcrafted lampshades also have custom filigree designs. «I like colors, and some shapes, to repeat through various design elements, and fortunately I have an excellent painter on my team who manages to achieve eye-catching results.»

The bedcoverings in this house – and in all those Sandy designs – are a true delight. «The cloth is Italian, of natural fibers, with luxurious details like lace on the sheets and many of the pillowcases.»

Exotic details

There are four bedrooms in the house, one of them on the upper floor. All are safeguarded by heavy dark wooden doors, and all have fairly high beds so that views of the open sea, and of the desert, will not be lost. The ceilings are planned for the same purpose, and this premise carries through to the bathrooms. Fine stonework dances on the floors, and details clamber up the walls.

Except in one room: completely lacking a view, it was painted, with a tropical landscape on one wall that is very jungle-like, «very Bali».

The circular staircase appears, with its narrow windows that trimly outline views of the desert, the spirit-soothing clouds, and a bit of the sea. The stairs lead to a room similar to the rest, but different; alike in form, different in its exotic details.

The wall décor consists of photographs by Tomás Spangler, large digitally-manipulated prints depicting very Mexican scenes and moods; these are interspersed with the generously-proportioned mirrors in their varied frames.

«What lies within...»

«The motivation for the interior design was that it should convey a bit of California and a bit of Mexico, but the most important goal was to have a house that was calmly balanced.» For that reason, the touches of blue were arranged one at a time and «little by little».

Sandy designed the entire project, from the floors to the bath and kitchen fixtures: starting from scratch, she walked in and beautified the home, and if a future owner wishes, she can continue on until it is left totally furnished, ready to set up housekeeping.

The living rooms that Sandy designs are divided into two or more zones, together but separate, friendly but distant. «This is done to allow people to pass through and head outdoors, without interrupting any conversation that might be going on in the room.»

When creating furniture arrangements, she likes for them to «share materials and dimensions, but for each piece to have its own character.» This happens with the room's sofas, chests and end tables: they seem related but there are no identical twins.

Unapologetically she accepts that antiques hold a special charm for her, and she manages to have all design elements communicate the same message of perfect balance, even when there are centuries of difference in their ages.

The house speaks of meticulousness, of someone who lingers over the smallest details. It is left for us to discover, for example, that the colors of the bed sheets are echoed in the painted walls and the tones of the bath, or to wonder at the way fabrics in curtains, cushions, armchairs and sofas all complement one another.

California and Mexico have no problem co-existing in this home; the ocean brings them together in a warm relationship that is impervious to air, wind and fire.

It looks very Mexican, with roof tiles and local stone contributing to the effect. Inside, there is a more international feeling, where harmony prevails.

CASA
Mis Amores

Casa Mis Amores:
A place where there is plenty of time to think glad thoughts

Walter and Diana Staudinger
OWNERS

Gunter Frissen
DEVELOPER

Architect Jaime Barba
PROJECT

Architect Guillermo Morfín
PROJECT ASSISTANT

A path hidden in the jungle outside of Sayulita, Jalisco brings us to a proud and self-possessed place surrounded by gardens, manzanilla and ficus trees. The two social areas, living room and dining room, are roofed with enormous palapas, each having its silk-bladed fan to provide caressing breezes.

Gunter Frissen says that «the land is like a big movie that is there to watch time and time again.» It shapes and re-shapes itself to resemble an embrace on the beach.

This house has several magical spaces, unique in their simplicity and tranquillity: the tennis court with an unimpeded view to the water along its own shore; the bath, standing amidst greenery, pleased with itself as it offers a lofty outlook to anyone occupying the toilet; the humble garden palapa, and the private virgin beach.

Good vibes

A fallen tree trunk announces that you've arrived at the house, and a plump wooden face spitting water in the middle of a tree establishes the mood of playfulness that is repeated throughout all the property's vertical and horizontal planes.

«99% of the vegetation that deserved to be, was respected. In place of the weeds, we planted *potentilla* seeds – a species native to this zone of western Mexico. Plants of the region were used to restore the estate to an ecological balance which had to a certain degree been lost.

The vestibule opens to an uninhibited welcome. It has two half-baths to accommodate visitors. This is a residence like many

The owners are German and the house, boldly Mexican. It must be seen face-to-face, in order to completely appreciate it.

beach-homes, with a an unequivocal interest in parties, in guests, in sharing itself. It can be found performing its domestic functions every day of the year; when there are no residents on hand, there is still maintenance and cleaning going on.

«I wanted to work with Mexican design concepts, some of them reminiscent of ethnic styles, and I wound up with a mix between the tropical style of the Careyes coast here on the Pacific, and the motifs of Teotihuacan (the archaeological site whose famous Pyramids lie just outside of Mexico City) – all crafted by artisans.»

It has five bedrooms. One of them, the one on the main floor at the far right, has a terrace shaded by a manzanilla tree, which in summertime is home to the land crabs, and at times even provides a place for humans - this is its high season though, and it's a case of first-come, first-served.

Down further, between the garden and the beach, is the meditation area, where nothing distracts the mind, nothing interferes with the free flow of one's thoughts.

Subtle luxury

The landscape is adorned with graceful walls in the colors of the sunset. The building rises in a natural clearing in the terrain, and clumps of vegetation divide the surroundings in both directions: fragments of walls and palapas are seen from every angle, and the same kaleidoscope effect happens with the sea and the sky.

«I delivered the house furnished, with just a few things missing, but otherwise ready to live in.» Gunter designed the furniture, and feels lucky to have had the opportunity to create a first project of such scope. He likes the look of iron at the edge of the sea, accepting the humidity without becoming nonplussed, acquiring a patina that becomes an extra benefit, an additional beauty; so he has made sure there is plenty of it.

The bedrooms all have telephones, satellite TV, full baths, dressing room closets, a small kitchen with the essentials for the good life, and of course views.

Each one has all the advantages, though the master bedroom, right above the vestibule, has a shade more of everything than the rest. In addition, there are two villas in the garden, located with more independence and celebrating total freedom in their building design.

The tennis court is joined by another palapa, whose center is occupied by a kind of fountain – which actually turns out to be nothing else but an icebox of major proportions, for impromptu

It is seriously spacious, and no home could offer
more privacy. Alone on the sandy coast,
it is surrounded by jungle.

parties. With such details the house sends a single eloquent message: here one must enjoy life everywhere on the property, and at all times.

Delicacy

It is a building that does not turn you loose very easily, insisting on holding onto its human inhabitants – try to leave, and you run right into its next game, at which your presence is required.

The facilities are hidden, «as I believe they must be when you have a landscape like this; and the purpose is not only to leave the view unobstructed, but to protect things like cables and circuitry.»

Interwoven manzanillas measure out the stunning view as it filters through whimsically-formed branches, smooth rolling grass, many-colored flowers. «With so much sea, one asks, 'what co-mes next?'»

A part of the beach is covered with a wild grass that cures jellyfish stings, «so I left it there, as a natural first aid kit.»

Casa Mis Amores is the greatest challenge with which Frissen has been presented, «a challenge to mature as a person, which is what I always wanted to do. Now I'm ready for this, and for whatever comes next.» And for Gunter there are still spaces left to invent: «Up there on a hill there's a 360-degree view to be had, where it would be possible to build a palapa, further on, a place for picnics, and even a bit further along, a nudist area.» He remembers, gratefully, that the owners agreed that they shouldn't be allowed to visit the property during the last months of the work. He sent videos to them to report on progress. He knows he was privileged to have this time and values the experience, all of which leaves him no room for false pride.

A lifelong guest

Before the estate was purchased by its current owner, there lived on this land an Italian, in his «country house». His name is Vito and he lives in his own little universe. He is 70 years old and devotes himself exclusively to meditation. He didn't like it when they arrived to build the house, he moved down to the beach, he disappeared. Gunter found him one day on another homestead, and invited him to return. A deal was struck and now he occupies a small area of the private beach. Don Vito has no intention of returning to Italy – nor to the real world. His presence is an endorsement, from a certified resident of the paradise that is Mis Amores.

Something for every taste, and every state of mind;
from the austere meditation terrace
to the tennis courts which look out to sea.

Villas del Mar

VILLAS DEL MAR: ITS DISTINGUISHING FEATURES ARE HIDDEN WITHIN

KEN SCHNITZER AND RON HATFIELD
VILLAS DEL MAR
DEVELOPERS

SANDY ESPINET
INTERIOR DESIGN

The development is a concept in vacation homes that is unique to the Los Cabos region. Although it is no longer new, its standards remain true to their original intent. The homes' designs have been modified at one stage or another, always in accordance with market demand, which asks for more and more: more bedrooms, more square meters, more spaciousness.

All the exteriors are similar, adhering unconditionally to a master plan which confers harmony and homogeneity upon the subdivision, leaving its residents in comfortable anonymity. Clients who buy houses which are already finished may make certain changes; to the flooring, perhaps, the bathroom tiling, or the wooden cabinetry.

The owners of Villa Johnson, for example, wanted something that would remind them of Texas while at the same time assuring them that they were in Mexico, and they wanted blue as the predominant tone.

General overview

When leaving the street where all the neighbors look alike, one enters Villa Johnson's hallway - which is twice the expected height. The iron railings of its staircase lead past a long window, which follows the ascent and descent of the steps. On the wall there is a display of Texan hats, hanging from ox-yokes which have been converted to hatracks.

The Johnsons like antiques, along with pieces that are not too venerable, and some furniture that only appears to be old. In the living room there is a pair of chairs from seventeenth century Spain, and another pair originating in China. The dining room table was long ago conceived to serve as a worktable in a church.

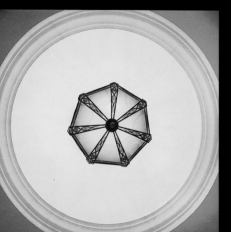

The little things

«When I deliver a house, I've added everything necessary: flowers, personal utensils, food. It is what is called a «turnkey» transfer, meaning that all that's needed is to open the door and walk in.» That is the level of attention that Sandy Espinet bestows upon her projects, and it creates quite an effect.

In addition to the quality of its construction and unsurpassed building lots, the advantage of this development it is that owners can leave whenever they wish to, without even switching off the air conditioner or emptying the refrigerator. Villas del Mar staff are in charge of closing, cleaning, and putting things back in their exact places – they do this by means of a photographic registry which prevents any errors – as well as installing hurricane protection, handling upkeep and maintenance on vehicles, getting everything in readiness again when the owners announce they'll be returning, even picking them up at the airport. And while the owners are in Los Cabos, all they have to do is call the management office if they want a massage, pedicure, chef, bilingual secretary, groceries or the newspaper delivered, any desire that might occur to them.

At Villas del Mar the finest materials are used, with such good taste that it pleases the most demanding clients, those who are accustomed to having the best. Sandy says that when she enters a villa to fine-tune the details, to guess at the wishes and whims of the owners, her work is simple: «what's difficult is deciding upon a focus, as there are so many options.»

More and more

There are many other homes like Villa Johnson. Villa Schnitzer, another of the large properties, is handled with serious design principles, but without a trace of monotony. It has two rooms on its ground floor and three on the second storey. It is distinguished by the elegance of its decoration and the formality of its rooms. Nothing betrays what occurs inside, that is only known by its proud owners and their fortunate guests.

Villa Sosin, on the other hand, declares its positive attitude toward relaxation even on the outside. In a daring but measured way, it avoids the tried-and-true without being actually provocative. Its tranquil style is enlivened by some glints of madness.

All share uniform elements:
tile roofs, quarry stone, arches, lattice,
and impeccably white walls.

Another pair of residences take fun as their guiding principle. In them, rules are broken outright. Each devises its own version for recreating their owners' particular lifestyle. They aren't cluttered with gaudy colors, figures or textures. A painter and her family vacation in one of these, an art collector in the other.

The impressions that each creates leaves anyone who might cross their thresholds breathless, but with a big smile on his or her face. Everything imaginable, as well as things that have never been dreamed of, calmly settles down upon multicolored sofas, or hangs itself upon design-filled walls. Strange details co-exist with shamelessly refined antiques.

In the whole panoply of villas there is just one property that has not even one set of arches. It has the hauteur to deal exclusively in right angles: from its porch to its jacuzzi all is perfectly square, clean lines without a hint of curvature.

Though it follows a different direction, its materials are all regulation: It neither eschews latticework nor quarry stone columns, roof tiles nor immaculate white walls.

The Casitas, «little houses» that are not small at all, sit on a mountaintop and are painted i earth tones. Greater privacy, and a wider view, compensate for their lack of beachfront.

Every one is self-sufficient – in accordance with the Villas' shared design edicts –, and each is possessive of its location.

All in all, Villas del Mar provides just those elements that its homeowners demand; in a spirit of full service, and the highest quality.

All diversity and individuality
happens within these villas: doors open
upon an explosion of design contrasts.

A basic principle unites them;
aside from the aspect of sameness,
quiet but impressive luxury is the driving force.

JULIO LÓPEZ
DESIGN AND CONSTRUCTION

Conscious of its setting, it makes no attempt to compete: rather, the home's intention is to be as unobtrusive as possible. In order to further conceal its existence, the stone used on its façade is a material that has been especially brought in from outside the region.

Though not a humble dwelling, it possesses a spirit of simplicity. Julio López, who is responsible for Casa Marcy's design and construction, does not want his projects to make any impact on the environment: instead, he works to imitate nature's forms, textures and colors.

Upon arrival

There are a pair of rocks in the entryway, part of the welcome and a continuation of the neighboring hill. In the same spirit of blending with the surroundings, it was decided that only desert plants should appear in the garden, which is stark but eloquent.

The stone that covers much of the façade was chosen for its potential to integrate the walls with the landscape, and to lend

shades and tones to the house. «The less you notice, the better,» Julio assures us as he explains his architectural stance. He says that it is preferable for the main impact to be found within, in the modernity and technology of the interiors, which are «totally automated.»

The house is discreetly situated to face the Pacific's clean and open horizon. Thanks to the topography, rooms were created with ten-foot ceilings, rooms where fresh air, light and landscape all coexist without unsettling the residents.

Julio López built them «a refuge which faces nature's immensity, but to human scale,» a home which gives them a feeling of pride and good fortune as they enjoy its space, its view, each of its comfortable rooms, and the practical arrangement that ties them all together.

The interpreter

«I am not one of those who makes the house he wants, and then hopes the owners will adapt to the space.» Julio notes that when he stands at the site, it is the land that tells him what he can do there; the clients outline their needs, and the terrain demonstrates its possibilities.

«When I've gotten to know the building lot, I listen to what the owners would like, and we determine how far their budget will go. At times I find myself with proposals for areas that are not workable or advisable, and then I begin negotiating between what the owners want and what can actually be done.» Julio is self-taught; while he has followed his own course of architectural

studies, he has been building «according to intuition and family inheritance» for many years.

Especially with this house, he was always aware, in every sketch he made, of the residents' infirmities; because of these he designed the space with minimal ascents and descents, few stairs. It is one thrusting «length along the horizontal.»

What you see...

Nothing is hidden, nothing is glossed over. From the beginning, when the main door first opens, everything is here: house, sky, sea, desert, «in one fell swoop», without visual legends or complex codes to decipher. A closet is a closet, a bathroom a bathroom, without any arcane design vocabulary. The façade presents a very clean line, and all the rest – pool, terrace, patios – seem to be carved from the very terrain, sometimes ending at a fixed point, but in many other places flowing here and there.

The living room, dining room and kitchen appear as soon as you cross the threshold. They occupy a floorplan nearly fifty feet long by approximately twenty feet wide. A very spacious first storey, which stretches from one side of the lot to the other. Each room is as important and as ample as the next, without playing favorites; each has the forthright mission of welcoming friends. The kitchen is not undervalued because of its utilitarian function, it is warm and hospitable. The master bedroom and one of the guestrooms are located at the far right on this level, both with doors onto the pool.

At the far left end of the living room, two staircases open up: the one on the right leading to the garages and a patio for cleaning the day's catch, «thus avoiding any wafting of fish odors through the main house.» The stairs on the left – more rounded, with greater depth – take one to a pair of guest bedrooms, with a bath and small kitchenette. Each has its own private balcony and view of the sea.

The hill fits itself to the inner landscape, appearing through the windows and reflected in the textures of the house.

The patio takes its organic forms from the land it rests upon, making a sensible break with the angular rigidity of the walls. «I like movement that generates shadows, and am not a fan of extreme straightness, but prefer to turn and see the mountain, the sunset.» Julio adopts the region's colors and constructs his homes with them, redesigning the landscape to include the architecture.

Mixing right angles, clean surfaces
and pleasing curves, the house demonstrates
a simple wish to fit with its setting.

CASA *Summitt*

CASA SUMMITT: SERIOUSLY MEXICAN, WITHOUT ARTIFICE OR OVER-SUBTLETY

JIMMY AND BARBARA SUMMITT
OWNERS

JUAN PABLO STONE
CONSTRUCTION

Starting at the gate that marks off the boundaries of the property, Casa Summitt dons its regional dress and invites us to enter a patio where a central quarry-stone fountain is surrounded by large clay-potted palms. From there, we are led on a journey through forms and backgrounds which at times contradict one another, but which always join to create a welcoming space.

«Client satisfaction is most important, it is everything,» notes Juan Pablo, adding that this property was Mr. Summitt's own dream: a house that would be «Mexican to the max».

The construction in the entryway, for example, is not merely tinged with Mexican style; it is completely faithful to the model which inspired it. Corridors run off to each side, occasional tables and armchairs furnish the area, plants sit in clay pots, lanterns illuminate seaside evenings – all details reminiscent of an hacienda. The large house abounds with semi-circular arches, wrought iron railings, rustic wood and leather chairs, traditional curved roof tiles: its ample spaces are well-integrated, and ideally-proportioned. It adheres absolutely to the dictum, «when in Rome, do as the Romans do,» reproducing the layout and dimensions of a prosperous Mexican gentleman's country home, except that this estate is located facing the surf, atop a cliff that adds a touch of drama to its general mood of warmth and composure.

Total contrast

Its rooms are generous and its ceilings high, some vaulted and others supported by strong beams of dark wood. The corridor's arches are white, but their starkness is tempered with a brickwork cornice.

When the sun is behind the clouds, a pair of wood and leather settees with indigo-blue upholstery drowsily keep each other

*The patio at the center and the passageways
along the perimeter bespeak a typical house
in an old village, except that hidden
behind this country home there is the ocean.*

company on the lawn – one example of Mr. Summitt's distinctive goal, which was to come to Mexico and live like a Mexican, while at the same time enjoying the beautiful seascape, the ocean breezes, the musical murmur of the tides. This intention became a home where Mexican life is not only visual but also tactile, and in constant motion. «What makes the house work so well is the main axis that divides the vestibule, patio, living room, pool and terrace.»

Anywhere one chooses to look, there are objects, settings, colors and textures that faithfully reproduce a very precise style. A wooden archangel looks defiantly at guests from his stand in an indirectly-lit niche. When night falls, lanterns create such a lush play of shadows that we feel as if we were being shown an updated version of the striking skies for which Mexican cinematographer Gabriel Figueroa was so famous.

The staircase is almost monastic, with an open candelabra whose dozen tapers light the way to prevent stumbling, and not incidentally to shine upon the dense and earnest yellow patina of the walls. The upper floor has a hallway along its perimeter, it has lanterns, it has wrought iron railings, and – so that it may lack absolutely nothing in the way of Mexican country style – it has strong cylindrical wooden columns that permit the roof to be set with decorative tiles.

With the sun's warmth

All the elements called for by the surroundings, and by the coastal weather, appear in the garden: a pair of palapas, a swimming pool, and a thatched yellow wall. Here the sea wins a sporting match, and the property yields to become a part of the beach, nothing more nor less. At the house's rear elevation, the sea and sand offer no quarter, but the house fights valiantly for center stage: which it gains after all, because it is impossible to imagine the scene without its proudly constructed projections, balconies and terraces.

In short, «the house is of fine quality, it is spacious and comfortable.» Fourteen months in being built, it meets with the approval of its owners and satisfies their dedication to Mexican design.

Mexican personality and taste permeate all its rooms, never distracted by the pride of place its setting inspires.

The wood and leather seats facing the surf sum up the owner's way of life, as do the wrought iron, the columns, all the décor.

Las Alamandas

ISABEL GOLDSMITH
OWNER

This is a highly select paradise, admitting only twenty-eight guests at a time. Each privileged visitor gains access to a realm in the midst of lush foliage – the resort takes its name from the golden flowers that bloom prolifically here. It is a world of formal balance, subtle settings, and most of all, privacy – made exceptional by luxury in the most literal sense of the word.

The architecture accords closely to the local style of the Careyes coast, where palapas are an outstanding design element, where paths lose themselves in their own twists-and-turns and those of the surroundings, and where the colors of the walls declaim an ode to well-being. Each walkway is decorated with designs crafted in stones of variegated hues, which combine to create mariner's compasses and true-to-life dolphins splashing through their own watery element.

The sense of well-being does not impose, it simply flows from the formula created by owner Isabel Goldsmith. An article published in *The New York Times* four years ago noted that only the daughter of a multimillionaire could have conceived, and built, a project like this one. And it's true, Isabel is the daughter of Sir James Goldsmith, a prominent British businessman, and the granddaughter of Atenor Patiño, «the tin baron»: she knows how to live well with certain advantages, and in Las Alamandas she has faithfully replicated her system for ease and splendor.

Nature per se

They are six villas, 14 suites, set upon an enormous estate that is splashed by the Pacific Ocean and the San Patricio River. The fulfillment of a guest's dreams can be ordered «a la carte», and requests are granted with discretion and efficiency.

*Deep within, this property holds
the key to living in luxury; a luxury
such as is known by only a select few
of the most elite. Those who know,
know it by heart, and have known it forever.*

Each area has everything that a guest might require, to such a degree that «require» is hardly the word: there is so much on offer here that it strains even the most vivid imagination. A picnic, a horseback ride, an intimate candlelit dinner, a mountain bike excursion, a tennis match or a golf game..., all you have to do is ask. And all these activities take place within ephemeral walls, in open spaces blown by salt breezes, or on golden sands where no one is around to distract from the horizon.

The staff persons that attend to one's wishes – or guess them even before they are expressed – are clothed impeccably in white, so as not to disturb the resort's careful chromatic scheme: colors are confined to a few walls, a niche here and there which appropriates the Mexican pink of the bougainvilleas, the orange that burns in the sunset, or the blue that gleams on a starry night. Colors also glow in the examples of Mexican craftsmanship arranged throughout Las Alamandas – handmade bowls, jars and vases, as well as textiles.

The garden furniture does not sacrifice comfort; a lounge next to the pool has the same proportions as the bed in the guest's room. Armchairs also play an important role: they sit upon the terraces, are scattered about the lawn, and are always poised on the beach for guests to comfortably await the setting of the sun.

In the middle of nowhere

Isabel opened the hotel in 1990. The estate could accomodate hundreds of guests, but she prefers that there be just a few strolling through her property at a time.

The care of the greens and greenery, the suites and common areas, is as scrupulously managed as the service offered to visitors – by a staff of 85. Nothing departs from the course laid out for elegant hospitality, nothing happens without its being part of the master plan.

Las Alamandas is located between Manzanillo and Puerto Vallarta. There is not much here to declare its presence; it prefers to be discreet in a way that reflects its good upbringing, and takes subtle pride in its heritage.

A taste for Mexico, put at the service
of just a few inhabitants.
Every corner of this large property
exudes an air of intimacy and cosmopolitan style.

Our special thanks
to the following people for the collaboration
which made this book possible:

RUBÉN ÁLVAREZ IBARRA

JACINTO ÁVALOS

JAIME BARBA

LEÓN CABRERA ESQUENAZI

ANTONIO CARRERA T.

JORGE CARRERA T.

SANDY ESPINET

ÓSCAR ESPINOSA ALÍ MODAD

GUNTER FRISSEN

ENRIQUE GARCÍA ÁLVAREZ

ALIX GOLDSMITH

ISABEL GOLDSMITH

ELIA LUZ GONZÁLEZ

MOHAMED AND YOLANDA HADID

JOHN AND CLARA HARTESDY

AL KAIRIS

JULIO LÓPEZ

JUAN MANUEL MUNGUÍA

JAIME OCHOA QUIÑÓNEZ

GUSTAVO ORTIZ DE ZÁRATE

RICARDO RODE

JUAN PABLO STONE

JIMMY AND BARBARA SUMMITT

PRÓSPERO TAPIA

CYNTHIA AND ALEJANDRA TAPIA

MIGUEL TORRES

CATHERINE ANN DOLLY WEBER KOHLER

GEORGE AND CLAIRE WEISS

RICK WESSELINK

DON AND ALICE WILLFONG

Houses by the Sea was printed in February, 2003, in Hong Kong, by Global Interprint, Inc. It is set in Carleton and Eras fonts. Printed on 150 gram weight couché gloss paper. 1st edition of 3000 copies.